AND WHILE
YOU'RE HERE

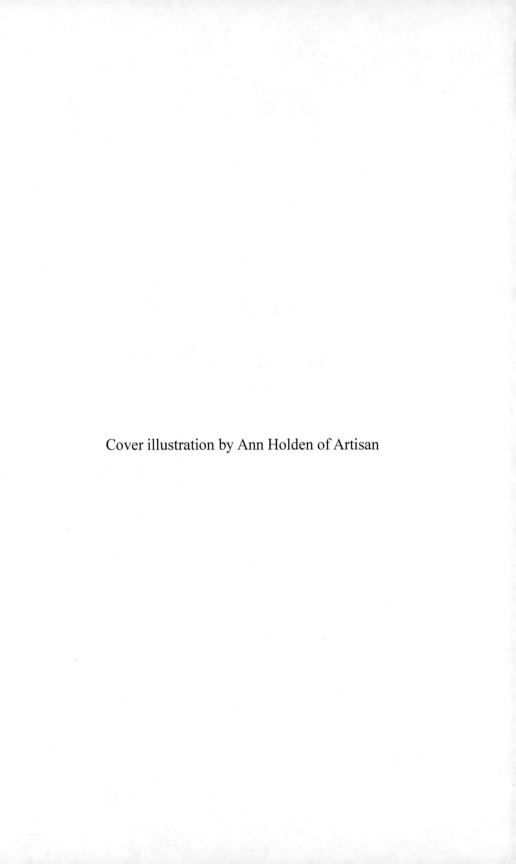

Cover illustration by Ann Holden of Artisan

AND WHILE YOU'RE HERE

Episodes in a Vet's Life

DR ANDREW EDNEY

authorHOUSE®

AuthorHouse™
1663 Liberty Drive
Bloomington, IN 47403
www.authorhouse.com
Phone: 1-800-839-8640

First published by AuthorHouse   31/10/2011

ISBN: 978-1-4567-8854-4 (sc)

Printed in the United States of America

Contents

Dedicated to
Sydney George and
Dorothy Mary Edney

Foreword

There comes a time in most of our lives when most of us think we should write our life story. This is not just so that we can be recorded for ever but to remember the best bits while we can still remember them. Enough exciting, amusing and frightening experiences happen in our veterinary lives. We don't have to make them up.

I am grateful for the help and advice of many colleagues, especially Mike Nelson, Raymond Hurt, Dean Smith, Barbara Knight and Ann Holden of Artisan for the cover picture.

When I was thinking of embarking on this enterprise I happened to sit at the Bar of the Golden Fleece pub in the market square of Thirsk in North Yorkshire with James Alfred Wight. I had gone there to present an Award to this famous veterinarian who we all knew as Alf. He published in the name of James Herriot. As with many great characters he didn't talk much about his own work. He was very interested in what I had been doing. When I said I was thinking of writing my life story he was most encouraging. When I said I was worried as I thought it would be rather episodic. His immediate reply was that 'all life is episodic', and so it is; especially in our profession.

We agreed that the title 'While You're Here' would ring bells with all who do house calls. Be it builders, electricians, plumbers and the like. In our case you may have gone on a visit allowing about 10-15 minutes to sex the cat or parrot. When you have completed the task the awful words 'Oh and while you're here . . . 'could ask you to attend the wildebeest in the garden, or whatever. It usually tends to take twice as long as the original appointment, and it can be more hazardous.

I have to admit that I have even imposed this on visiting workers at my house.

Chapter 1

Early Days:
How Did I Get Into This?

'What do you want to be **if** you grow up?' said my father, a schoolmaster. 'I want to be a doctor' I said, largely because I thought that was what he wanted to hear. 'You've got the handwriting for it already' was his immediate response.Up to that point, when I was about eight years old, I hadn't shown much evidence of intellect or the will to do any work at all. There was a war on after all.

My handwriting remains distinctly medical. My explanation for this is that some years earlier we had been evacuated and moved from a school which had yet to teach joined up writing. When I did eventually finish up in a full time school, the class I was in had already been groomed in basic calligraphy. As computer technology has advanced it has allowed me to record my thoughts without my readers having to seek help from the Bletchley Park school of code breakers. It was clear though that I was not alone in my Jackson Pollock style writing. A point well illustrated when, as a student I got an exam paper back with comments from the examiner which were completely unreadable. I asked the person concerned what the scribble actually said. It was decoded as 'Has done quite well but would get much better marks if his handwriting was more legible'.

Apart from a few remaining school reports, most of the early days of my career can only be recalled from memory. However, as this included all of the World War II period, those memories are especially well etched. On the rare occasions when there is a bout of insomnia threatening, I have found that a sure-fire cure is to review in sequence every event in your life you can put a date to. It works for me and I am in the land of slumber by the time I was sent off to primary school. One easily dated event was the historic broadcast by Prime Minister Neville Chamberlain on the 3rd September 1939. We all gathered round the wireless set (radio) to hear that 'We are now at war with Germany'. We children were young enough to treat it all as a lark, at least in the early part. Despite the fact that both my father and grandfather were heavily involved in the First World War, it meant very little to me. In common with many survivors of that harrowing episode, the subject was never discussed, even though my grandfather had been awarded the Military Cross. I am still trying to track down the details of the circumstances. All I have been able to discover is that it followed a mustard gas attack when all the others died and he didn't, so he got the medal. That was the family story. Many adults of my vintage have similar thoughts on how their existence was the result of their ancestors survival against the odds.

Within a very short time my brother and I had become evacuees. We lived in the Medway towns where there was a large naval dockyard, two aircraft factories and Army and Royal Marines bases. The area was an obvious target for the Luftwaffe. We had to be moved to the country. We went with my father's school so our family stayed together. My school was evacuated to a location on the Channel Coast near Dover. This seemed strange as once France was occupied you could almost see the Germans from there some twenty miles away. In fact rather than just a simple bombing, which was inflicted on most of the South East of England, Dover was shelled from across the Channel. We got on a train in Chatham, complete with gas masks and labels and disembarked some ten miles down the line. Father was the Billeting Officer for his school. He took his party of some twenty very young children and knocked on the doors of the houses on his route. Each occupant was asked how many bedrooms they had and were told to take one or two children from the group, depending on their response. They were then required to point to the ones they would take on. As I was at the front, fingers pointed at me in many cases. My parents assumed that this was because I was cute. My opinion was, and still is that it was because I was simply at the front. This is something that caused me to stand at the back whenever possible for the rest of my childhood. Surprisingly though, this extraordinarily cavalier approach to allocating very young boys, was mostly very successful. Some life-long friendships resulted in many cases. Many still remain good friends. There was a war on you know. If there were disasters, the information was withheld from the general public. It would have damaged morale.

The first few days were chaotic. We collected our 'iron rations' from the local grammar school and went to share the accommodation of a couple of elderly ladies. One appeared to be semi-conscious much of the time and the other was on oxygen supplied by way of a mask from a cylinder. They had a housemaid and a wonderful Red Setter called 'Myrna'. She triggered my initial interest in animals. We struck up an immediate rapport; at last there was someone who understood me, the dog that is. In a couple of days, the first siren sounded so we all crowded under a sizeable oak table. We expected to be bombed out immediately, but it turned out to be a false alarm. The Setter had what appeared to be a premonition, before each subsequent raid she made straight for the gate-leg table well before the siren went off. I now realise that she had very acute hearing and could pick up the sounds from sirens along the chain from the coast.

We moved into our own house on Christmas Eve of that year. We had gone from Canterbury Street in Gillingham to Canterbury Road in Sittingbourne. Clearly we were moving up in the world. The house was however close to the direct route the Luftwaffe took on their way up to London. So we had almost a front row seat to see both the Battle of Britain and of the nightly bombers that delivered the blitzkrieg on London some forty miles away.

Schooling was somewhat improvised for the first year or so. We had classes in a variety of buildings in town. These included a fish and chip shop in East Street, the Shakespeare's Head hostelry nearby, the Methodist Church and finally the Mission Room. Classes were each divided into two groups. Half were taught in the mornings and the other half in the afternoons. I was in the afternoon section, which probably explains why I am definitely not a morning person. We discovered later that the reason for this strategy was, apart from staff shortages, that if the school room was hit, only half of us would be killed. In the event the only damage we experienced was the ceiling of my bedroom being brought down by a land mine exploding. The only injuries I sustained were a slight bruise or two being blown into our Anderson shelter by a VI 'doodlebug' and when I skewered my foot with a garden fork when we were filling in a hole in the ground after we had decommissioned the shelter. I was rushed off for an anti-tetanus injection, which really frightened me.

Being very young the real awfulness of the war was largely hidden from me. The hostilities we did see included some bombing but it was mainly aerial combat which took place overhead. We as children saw this as a display keeping us entertained. In the early years I would be taken down to our DIY air raid shelter at the bottom of our garden and remain fast asleep. I would be brought up again when the All Clear sounded unaware that I had even been moved. This could explain why I have little trouble sleeping, it's getting up that can be a problem. As the war progressed, we children amused ourselves by collecting trophies such as bullets, shrapnel and pieces of incendiary bombs. The flammable characteristics of the magnesium alloy heads of these items provided us with entertainment of an extremely dangerous and prohibited kind. We became very skilled at aircraft recognition. That is if the plane spiralling to earth in flames was 'one of theirs' or 'one of ours'. We would give a loud cheer if members of the crew took successfully to their parachutes if the latter.

A couple of experiences did start to bring home to me that there was more to it than the fun of watching aircraft engaged in complex manoeuvres overhead. For once I had stayed awake in the dugout shelter as we all waited for the church bells to ring out. Mercifully, they didn't. Had they done so, it would have signaled the expected German invasion. It was another four years before they were rung joyfully to celebrate the end of the war in Europe.

My brother Joseph being four years older than me, discovered the seriousness of the war we were watching much earlier than I did. One particular event changed both our lives. I can still see the Heinkel III bomber diving earthwards in a 'falling leaf' pattern, from around 600-800 feet, having been the prey of a Spitfire fighter which went into a 'victory roll' immediately afterwards. Joe went off on his bicycle to view the crashed raider. I was restrained from following as a result of being a little slow off the mark. The enemy aircraft fell to earth about four miles away, but what Joseph was not prepared for was the fact that the crew were still on board when it hit the ground. It blew to pieces and scattered human remains across the local cherry orchards. He returned ashen faced and never went again, neither did I.

The inconveniences of our trips to the air raid shelter during air-raids and food rationing were relatively trivial compared with the experiences of those in Central London at the height of the Blitz. We were only forty miles away and could see the very extensive fire storms there but were spared the direct effects.

These were familiar to us but even more gruesome events were taking place elsewhere in Europe and beyond.

Even so, one incident colours my memory permanently. My mental picture of that day was brought to the surface in spectacular fashion recently as I watched a television programme called 'Doodlebug Summer' I had recorded earlier that day. One stunning clip was no more than a minute or so in duration, but it left me thunderstruck. We saw pictures of a railway bridge which had been hit by a VI. That is the pilotless 'Vengeance weapon I' flying bomb known to us all as the 'Doodlebug'. It was as much a psychological device as an explosive weapon. Nevertheless one of them could wreck several buildings and kill many nearby inhabitants. The characteristic bubbling sound of their engine was heard every day. It was when it stopped that the effect was dramatic. It was a very frightening silence. You knew you had about half a minute to run for cover. The V2 came later but we were spared all but a few in our part of Kent. These were an early version of the rocket missile and there wasn't anything we could do to counter them at the time. They arrived without any warning at all. If the V weapons had been operating earlier in the war things would have been very different. I found out recently that the V2 Rocket had been tested by the Germans in 1942, two years before it was used.

Once our fighter aircraft such as the Tempest were fast enough to fly alongside the VIs, they deployed an effective technique. Instead of trying to shoot them down, the allied fighter would tip the doodlebugs wing over by air pressure from underneath. As a result its gyroscope would destabilise and the intruder would crash to the ground. Every one brought down in this fashion was one fewer to land on London. Unfortunately for us many of them exploded all round the Kent countryside. A total of 1,444 came down in Kent and around 1,000 in the Channel. We used to cycle up the North Downs to watch all this happening.

The person on the television programme told the story of his father surviving a train crash after a VI had hit the railway bridge at Upchurch on the 16th August 1944, but had died of a heart attack the next day. Although our small team of watchers of the 'Doodlebug War' had been up on the Downs that day and had seen this VI being brought down with a sizeable explosion, we were unaware that it had wrecked the railway bridge at Upchurch as the 4.45 train from Chatham approached. The trains engine and front carriages had gone across the bridge that wasn't there and seriously injured the engine driver and most of the occupants of the front carriages, some fatally.

When I got home that afternoon mother sent me off on my bicycle to the crash site as my father caught that train every day of his working life. He sat in 'his' seat in the front carriage as he completed the *Daily Telegraph* crossword in his usual apparently effortless fashion. By the time I got to the chaos at the bridge, police, ambulances, home guard and a few regular military persons were everywhere. I was not allowed very close as I was a young child but did manage to ask someone who appeared to be in authority what might have happened to my father. After some discussion I was told he was not on the list of those found dead or injured. It was made clear that they could not be certain. The fact that all had to carry identity cards at the time meant that the information they did have was probably reasonably reliable, although some cards could have been destroyed in the crash.

There was nothing else I could do and was told to get away from the site. So I had to slog the eight hilly miles back home to tell mother. It was much later that night when father came home complaining about all the problems he had had with the train service. There had been long waits for buses to be laid on. He had been umpiring a cricket match at his school so was not on his usual train. Cricket had saved his life.

When father did eventually retire, like most of us in that position he had very little spare time. Tending our garden kept us fairly self-sufficient. It was not long before a group of his former pupils turned up at our front door and pleaded with him to 'come back as we don't like the new headmaster'.

After a couple of years of fairly haphazard education interrupted by trips to the air raid shelter, I was sent off to the 'big school'. Prior to this one of my few educational highlights was winning a half crown postal order for writing an extremely jingoistic essay in a class competition. There was also an episode in the air raid shelter. This involved our teacher showing us how a short phrase passed along the line of benches (we were allowed to say this just once) transformed into something completely different by the time it got to the end of row three. This was in the style of the classic music hall version, 'Send me reinforcements we're going to advance' being changed to 'Send three and four pence we're going to a dance'. I can't remember the actual phrase we used, but it certainly illustrated the ease with which rumours were generated.

My performance at the big school was notable mainly for its mediocrity. We all wanted to be good at sport, for that was the way to be popular with class mates. My occasional (very) flashes of brilliance were not frequent enough to register in this way. I only made the cricket second eleven, albeit as captain, thus ruining my chances of getting into medical school. I eventually learned that the best way of getting on with those around you was to make them laugh, or at least to amuse them. This possibly explains why we often resorted to pranks of varying degrees of destructiveness.

All of this changed because of two people, Mr Ashby and Miss Moore. Although it was several years before we grew up enough to leave our pranks in the past. At an Old Boys Dinner recently as after dinner speaker I confessed that when I was in Form 3A 'I was in love with Miss Moore'. Those present of my vintage replied in unison 'Weren't we all?'. Our hormones were beginning to surge at the time that the lovely Joyce Moore came to teach us Latin and History and put them into fast forward. I even abandoned my strategy of sitting at the back of the class. The tussle for the front seats was a direct result of Miss M's habit of sitting **on** the desk instead of the usual practice of being seated behind it; and she had legs. Up to that time our only glimpses of the young female form had been sneaky peeps at hockey matches through the fence of the County School for Girls down the lane. Miss Moore became the main topic of discussion between our classmates. I gave up my desire for Jean Simmons for her.

I surprised myself and everyone else by taking a sudden interest in Latin and got quite useful at it. So much so that those in the class near me copied what I wrote. So, if I got it wrong I was in trouble all round. Then tragedy took over. A very handsome RAF Officer came to tell us all what a wonderful career we could have in the Royal Air Force. He took away our beloved teacher as his wife and they moved to Leicestershire. Being taught her subjects by Mr Jackson was just not the same, so our interests moved elsewhere. Mr Jackson's most memorable skill was being able to throw a piece of chalk with remarkable accuracy at anyone not paying attention.

As we moved on the class was expected either to go down the arts route or concentrate on science subjects. Us scientists thought the arts lot were rather wet. It was much more macho to peer down microscopes and learn the scientific basis for everything.

The great Mr Ashby was Deputy Headmaster. He opened my eyes to the biological sciences. He even encouraged us, making us believe that we could achieve a worthwhile life, rather than threatening us if we didn't 'try harder'. The rationale of this approach, comparable with the humane and effective method of dog training by reward and withholding reward rather than beating animals into submission took root in my mind.

One near disaster occurred when our Chemistry Master said to us that the date of one of our end of term exams had been 'put forward' a couple of days. What he should have said was it had been 'brought forward'. We argued with him saying that 'in the sequence of Monday, Tuesday, Wednesday . . . ., if you put a date forward two days it will be Friday, not Monday as it would be if you brought the date forward'. To our relief we won the argument and were spared punishment. Fortunately it was only an end of term exam so they dug out the exam papers and we sat it in a guarded place

Having done reasonably well in the School Certificate exams and gaining Matriculation we heard our Headmaster announce in clear tones to the morning assembly that those of us with such successful results could 'either take the Higher Course or the Inter Course'. Misunderstanding this completely we favoured the second, not realising that it was The Intermediate BSc course. A few of us went to Medway College to study 'Bot' and 'Zoo', that is Botany and Zoology whilst we continued at our home station with Physics and Chemistry. After two years, disaster supervened or rather what appeared to be a catastrophe at the time. But it is not always possible to tell that such setbacks could eventually prove to be beneficial. And so it turned out that failing Botany and not gaining my Higher School Certificate turned out to be a very well disguised blessing. Although I passed the other three subjects, that counted for nothing. I put this disaster down to the fact that we had to take these written exams at the Girls School for some reason and there were distractions. I did not answer a compulsory question.

As we moved from an unfulfilled desire to be Test Match cricketers, we entered a rather dreadful phase of carrying out pranks of progressive awfulness. These were mostly what we would now call vandalism. Much of the time we were well behaved, because the punishment was frightening. We never walked on the pitch of any sport if we weren't playing, we never argued with the referee or umpire and we never went on the railway line. I remember bending down to avoid a very fast cricket ball from a very quick bowler. The ball flew off my back and I was caught at first slip. I was given out by the umpire who either didn't see what happened or was on the other side. So I walked. One occasion did generate a murderous intent in me. The stumps went flying for the third time to complete what I thought was my first hat trick of three wickets as opening bowler, only to hear the umpire bellow 'no ball'. I knew it wasn't, but one didn't question authority then. Would it were still like that.

A third person was probably the most crucial influence on my future. Things would have been very different if it had been anyone else. As with many of our misbehaviours I was there when others did the dirty work. The others were 'Soapy' Watson, 'Nobby' Clarke and 'Smutty' Smith. We were at the end of our spell in the Lower Sixth Form. Soapy reckoned that any pranks would be blamed on the Upper Sixth who were at the end of their school days. We made sure that we were counted as being at the end of term assembly. We slipped craftily into the cloakroom only to be confronted by the legendry Mr Ashby. He told us to get back into the Main Hall without delay, but we didn't. Soapy appeared with a can of whitewash and a large brush. His target was our English master's Riley Monaco saloon car parked outside the front doors of the school. This beautiful motor had a fabric covered body, on which Soapy proceeded to spell out words in whitewash to the effect that its owner was 'Just Married'. However, his words proved too large for the space available and he had to amend it to a rather messy version of 'Just Wed'. As he was completing all this, the one person we had not taken into account came walking up the driveway. We all froze as the footsteps of Miss Millen crunched along the gravel path. Miss Millen, one of the worlds contraltos, was the Headmaster's very formidable Secretary. She was all powerful. There was no point in trying to run away as she had seen us all. There was a lengthy pause as she looked at the disfigured vehicle. She turned to us and in ringing tones said 'Oh but he has been married some time' and walked away. I just wanted to get out of the area but Soapy wanted to watch results from behind a fence nearby. He was quite right in that the Headmaster went straight to the group of the Upper Sixth who were leaving, and laid into them in no uncertain manner about the outrage. All summer we lived in terror of the coming term. Our classmates continuously reminded us of our predicament. To our amazement nothing happened, although we did not relax for many weeks for fear of being sent down on our return. We have Miss Millen to thank for being spared. I am sure she knew that if she 'split' on us we would be finished with regard to any claim to have any further education of any standard. No doubt she also worked out that we would have a very unpleasant period of not knowing our fate throughout the summer. That would surely be enough punishment. The thing I felt worst about though was that we had targeted the wrong member of staff. Mr Nicholls was another teacher who cared about his pupils. He introduced me to serious music, literature and fine art with enthusiasm and skill. These influences which remain with me, came to fruition during my experiences with the Open University many years later. Had he come along earlier I might have gone down the arts route at an early stage. But it was Miss Millen who saved my career; I'm sure Mr Ashby had a pretty good idea who the culprits were too.

Sports day saw a great deal of effort, with less than Olympic results. I did however, win one race. It was a case of 'the first will be last and the last will be first'; at least the way I played it it was.

As we came up to the finish I was trailing more than somewhat. I noticed as we came to the last few yards that those who thought they had won slackened off, allowing me to sneak in and win, 'many that are first shall be last; and the last shall be first' Mathew xix v30. I learned from that, never to give up.

When the Headmaster asked me what I wanted to do as a career, I said that I wanted to be a vet. His immediate response was to tell me loud and clear that 'I would never get into vet school'. I'd show him I thought. I did get a place, but it took rather longer than I had anticipated. Whether the Head said all this to make sure I didn't waste my time applying or to motivate me to go for it, I still don't know. I will have to give him the benefit of the doubt as he is no longer with us.

My leaning towards veterinary medicine began to crystallise following meetings with two cousins who were very equine in their outlook. One of their horses I rode when I was very young had serious steering problems. However, neither I nor the horse were injured. Cousin John and his sister Jo lived for all manner of equine activities and were very successful in the local events. Jo had spent some time with the local veterinarian. She had been praised for taking an active interest in the blood soaked details of a post mortem examination she had seen at a local farm. Praise was something I yearned for. So I decided to find out more about becoming a 'horse doctor'.

As I had done reasonably well in French, getting a credit when most thought that I would not even reach the pass mark, two of us decided to hitch-hike across France to try to reach the Mediterranean. We actually managed to get almost to Lyon. I doubt if we would get as far as Canterbury now. A serious drawback at the time was that the local population did not seem to have taken the same French lessons as us. They could not understand what I was saying much of the time. However, I did spot a headline in a newspaper being read by a person on the next table to us in a café in Mâcon. This was the first indication that National Service in Grande Bretagne was being extended from eighteen months to two years. Clearly they were not going to get enough out of me in one and a half years, or so I thought. The reality was that the Korean War had begun and we might have to take part in that. Six months is but a short fragment in time now, but then it seemed a quite a lengthy spell. It certainly upset those who were due to come back into civilian life and had a job set up.

Off I went for my medical, veterinary science would have to wait.

Myself at three days old, with brother Joseph seated alongside

Bring on the clowns. Father as Pierrot seated centre, circa 1920

Brother Joseph and myself at Rochester Castle

Just before 'The Day War Broke Out' in August 1939

Andrew on the way to winning The High Jump
at the school sports day

Upchurch railway bridge after the V1 explosion in 1944. Photograph
courtesy of The Kent Messenger.

Chapter 2

The Gap Years

Apart from a few days at a Boy Scout encampment and short visits to relatives, I had never been away from home. As a direct result of failing one of my Higher School Certificate exams and passing my medical examination A1, I was invited to join the Royal Air Force. In fact they were said to be quite pushy about it and there was no getting out. It turned out to be the best thing that happened to me up to that point.

About half way through the traditional traumas of 'square bashing' at RAF Padgate in Lancashire, a few of us were moved to Hornchurch in Essex for aircrew selection. This consisted of a week of quite demanding tests. Anyone who failed had to polish the windows and brass fittings throughout the base for the rest of the week. As a result of this the place sparkled more than anywhere else in Essex.

One of the many tasks we had to perform was in the form of a peg board. The square pegs were painted black at the top and white below. We had to demonstrate our manual dexterity by pulling them out and putting them back the other way up against the clock. There were about 50 pegs on each board and we were timed and observed closely. One candidate sitting next to me achieved the objective in seconds simply by turning the board over. I was annoyed that I had not thought of that until the Officer in charge went berserk and threw him off the course. So much for initiative I thought.

The survivors of the aircrew selection board were sent off to various RAF bases around the country. I found myself in what to me was the far North, that is Yorkshire where in RAF bases at Driffield and Leconfield we experienced fearsome January weather. I was beginning to wish I had stayed bashing the squares in Padgate.

Part of our aircrew training took the form of a short spell in a decompression chamber. This was to demonstrate to us the effects of oxygen deprivation. It certainly did that. We went into the chamber in groups of about ten and sat down while we were taken up to a simulated altitude by evacuating the oxygen to the level it would be at ten thousand feet and above. The rest of the group stood outside and looked in through small windows to observe our behaviour. We felt a little light-headed but no more as we gave our names and service numbers in turn. Things got a little more complicated as we stood up and sat down again to order and had to answer basic questions. Then we were ordered to start counting from one hundred, ninety nine, ninety eight and so on as we were progressively deprived of more oxygen. Few of us got beyond ninety when it all went blank. It was when we got to watch from outside the others go through this procedure that we saw how silly we all looked as we became more anoxic. This exercise made the point very well that without a supply of oxygen above 10,000 feet the crew were likely to become dangerously unreliable without knowing it.

Unfortunately, our group were taken one stage further by accident. We were at a simulated altitude of 30,000 feet and were wobbling all over the place, when the power went off and we were in total darkness. I have no idea how long this remained the situation. In fact I have very little memory of this part of the episode. We could only listen in amazement to the accounts from those watching us. Whether this destroyed any part of my brain matter, I don't know. It's probably too late to sue them now.

Eventually we were allowed home on a 48 hour pass. Getting back to base proved frustrating as we had mistaken St Pancras station for Kings Cross and missed our last train. We had to be back by 0630 hours or we would end up in the guard room. We did find a train going to York late that night so at least we could get to Yorkshire. We hitch-hiked all night from there and managed to get back to base just before the deadline, only to be immediately turned round to make our way to RAF Calshot on Southampton Water. I was never travel sick on the aircraft but suffered a great deal on the train back to London. On arrival in Calshot we were greeted by the sight of the beautiful flying boats moored near the Solent. We were to convert onto the Short Sunderlands so we became 'web footers'.

At last I felt at home as I had spent my early childhood in the Medway Towns where the Short Brothers flying boats were built. In fact it was a while before I discovered that aeroplanes could land on the ground as well as put down on the river. We say that marine aircraft alight rather than land, except for some amphibians which can do both. We once did a fly past over the Farnborough Air Show during which Air Traffic Control asked if we planned to land there. We let them know that we did not think that was wise.

The operational squadron we were eventually sent to was based in what is known as 'Little England Beyond Wales', Pembrokeshire that is. It is only in fairly recent times that I have realised how beautiful the coastline is there. It included Milford Haven a natural harbour on the scale of Sydney, Australia. During a recent squadron reunion at Pembroke Dock (PD), on enquiry I told one of the locals 'No I wasn't Welsh but I did grow up here'. She was surprised when I added 'Yes I was eighteen at the time and it took about three months'. After years of rather repressive schooldays it was a delight to complete our sex education with such delightful people. Not only did we get paid reasonably well, we received 'flying pay' in addition; and the prices of drinks in the Mess were very manageable. So much so that we would play silly drinking games and then go chasing girls in Tenby. It might have been more successful if we had done it the other way round. We were very popular on Sundays as, apart from the Chapel in town, there wasn't much going on. The only other bars that were open were the Labour and the Liberal Clubs. There was no Conservative Club. We entertained the ladies in our Mess and at The Astra cinema, which occupied the old dockyard church and was also open on a Sunday. Better than the Labour Club any day.

Particularly riotous evenings took place when we shared them with our Royal Naval colleagues from the dockyard adjacent to our RAF base. I'm sure I would have been in danger of drinking myself to death if I had stayed in the Air Force. One of our pilots, Johnny Warren had a very sexy two-seater sports car that four of us would cram into to go seeking thrills in the De Valance Dance Pavilion in Tenby. Not only was this a favourite location for all the young in the 1950s, it was still there when I went back recently. On our way back to Pembroke Dock one Saturday night it seemed as if our driver was having a go at the 'Tenby to PD world record for a small sports car' when it inverted into a ditch. By a remarkable miracle no one was hurt. I looked back at the wreckage and realised I must have climbed out of the windscreen space, the glass having been dispersed across the local countryside. This was not my only passage through a car windscreen, an exploit I will relate in due course. I certainly had no memory of doing so on this occasion. We were all remarkably sober on our eventual return to the Mess.

Most of our aviation activities were taken up with eight to twelve hour patrols over the Atlantic flying at fifty feet above the ocean. As with most flying it could be extremely boring, very frightening and sometimes exhilarating. The sight of Rockall after some eight hours of looking at the sea and not much else was truly memorable. Soon afterwards we flew into a monster electric storm with the air temperature at minus 10 degrees F, with no heating in the aircraft. My cup of tea froze in the my hand just South of Iceland as a flash of lightning blew off our radar scanners and made our compasses useless. This caused some anxiety. By chance though there happened to be another aircraft from our squadron nearby. This was very unusual as we normally patrolled alone. So we were shepherded home to Wales and safety.

At least the crew could move around on a large flying boat. There was a galley, ward room and a primitive toilet with an Elsan facility. Going into various bomber aircraft of the time located in aviation museums around the world gives one a marked sense of claustrophobia in comparison. Because we had a modest amount of space, I felt the team spirit of the crew was a comfort. Most crews were made up of veterans from World War II, some with impressive decorations, who had to work with us young National Servicemen.

Of the many memorable events which were crowded into the short period of my military service, there are two that are well worth recording. We used to go to Northern Ireland from time to time for training updates on what was known as 'The Guinness Refresher Course'. We arrived at RAF Castle Archdale to alight on Loch Erne at night. The flare path consisted of lights mounted on buoys. Our Squadron Commander was at the controls. Unfortunately he put down **on** the flare path, rather than the usually accepted method of keeping the lights to one side. The result was one of the floats crumpled on impact putting us in danger of over-turning. Each wing had a float to keep the aircraft upright in the water. Losing one meant that we had to go straight into our broken float drill. This is something the crew had trained for many times. It was an emergency as we had to keep the wing without a functional float out of the water. The way we did this was to climb out on to the other wing immediately or we would capsize. It worked but it was very cold and wet, it would have been much worse if we had been too slow. We repaired to the mess at Castle Archdale even more rapidly than usual.

A recent visit to one of my publishers at Canary Wharf in the London Docklands stirred another vivid memory. It was Battle of Britain Week when for some reason we joined the anniversary celebrations. We were sent to the Tower of London for a very memorable week.

I had only been on the squadron for a few months when we were detailed to fly down to the Capital in Sunderland PP115 'Charlie' in September of that year. My role throughout the trip was as lookout in the astrodome. We left Pembroke Dock in South Wales to fly to London by way of RAF Mountbatten at Plymouth to pick up a VIP or two. We took our familiar route past Caldy Island to follow the coast of Wales in an Easterly direction. Here our navigator advised us in his usual style to 'turn a little South'; he had been a pathfinder during the last war. We had to adjust our usual route which was to follow the line of the pier at Weston-super-Mare to pick up the flaming beacon at Fawley refinery for Calshot on Southampton Water. This time we had to point towards Plymouth. As we approached Plymouth Sound, RAF Mountbatten control gave us permission to put down in the harbour. A dinghy had cleared the area of any floating objects which might cause us problems. It had not seen the swimmer at about the point where we would have hit the water. I drew our Captain's attention to this and we went round again. No doubt the swimmer had never seen thirty tons of flying boat coming down within a few feet of his body before. He went off at a startling rate which would have given an Olympian athlete a serious challenge had one been around. After a quick circuit, we retraced our approach but the swimmer was nowhere to be seen.

About an hour later we found ourselves making our final approach to Limehouse Reach on the Thames near Docklands. Several marine craft dinghies had cleared what appeared to be a rather narrow stretch of the river for us to alight on. However, I had to draw our Captain's attention to some sizeable cranes in the docks which were approaching us at an alarming rate. Our leader mentioned that he had already seen them and was going round again. He put us down on the water in his usual highly professional style and we were soon making our way to Tower Bridge. It was only then that we spotted the crowds of spectators who all waved at us enthusiastically. Tower Bridge itself was raised, we assumed was to prevent the crowds dropping heavy gifts on us from a great height. Alternatively it could have been that they had no idea of the dimensions of our aircraft.

With the forward gun turret retracted, our Flight Engineer and Signaller secured us to a buoy and another member of the crew attached a substantial line to our stern. We were moored right beside Traitors Gate. A dinghy took us ashore to present ourselves at the Royal Fusiliers Mess in the Tower of London. We were well looked after by the Army during our stay and had a conducted tour of the

Tower the following day. We had a close look at the Crown Jewels and witnessed the Ceremony of the Keys. But as we were being shown to our quarters I asked where the bathroom was as we could all do with a good clean up. The reply by the mess steward was 'I dunno mate, I've only bin 'ere a fortnight'. What we all wanted to do though was to go 'on the town', which we did several nights running. This was said to be in order, provided we got back by midnight and we gave those on guard the password. If we could not do either, we would not be allowed back in. On our first night out we made it back with seconds to spare, only to find that none of us could remember the password. One of our number moved us to one side as he wondered if the guards always knew the password of the day. Well it was worth a try. 'What's the password then?' demanded the guard in rather irritated tones. 'Churchspire' we said, which was our squadron call sign at the time; and they waved us past! We made our way through the unlit passages of the Tower towards the Mess. We turned 'a little North' as our Navigator was want to say, at one of the spookiest places in the world, the 'Bloody Tower'. At this point a heavily armed guard leapt out of the darkness and screamed at us as to what we were doing there. That was as scared as I had ever been, but it made sure I remembered the security details next time out.

While all this happened in the last century, these events are clearly etched in my memory. I treasure the photographs as I am able to prove that I have been under Tower Bridge in an aeroplane, and quite legally too.

Although the Korean War was going on at this time, we were spared all that. Playing war games is quite dangerous enough, without having to do it for real. The really crazy thing at the time was that I actually wanted to go out and see some action as many of my fellow aircrew had seen serious action in the last conflict and they had *medals*. This improved our chances with the women who liked men in uniform. By the time the Suez crisis came along, I had grown up sufficiently to be relieved that I did not have to risk my life for my country.

We occupied ourselves with practice bombs and did perform the first post war tests dropping live depth charges. This was well away from being any danger to the public. We were once sent off on an 'Air Sea Rescue' search which we thought was genuine but turned out to be an old wooden bed and mattress floating in Cardigan Bay. We didn't get any medals for that.

Another disappointment was when a piece of Radar equipment caught fire as we flew over Madeira. We all thought we would have a nice stay on the island, but the Captain had other ideas. He got us to throw the piece of kit out of the galley hatch and we returned to Gibraltar. Just as we were about to disembark we heard loud cannon fire from the mainland. The shots were repeated at minute intervals fifty four times. The King had died while we were away and the military were firing the cannons in his honour. The Mess was virtually closed for about a week.

As my two years in the services came to an end I applied to The Royal Veterinary College for a place and was summoned for an interview. The interrogators seemed impressed by the fact that I had played cricket for the Squadron and one even wanted to know about marine aircraft. He asked me to say what I thought was special about flying boats. My innate reticence was swept away as I launched into a eulogy. 'Why are they safer than other planes?' he asked. I said that I would rather be in one that floats when over the sea than in a plane that 'ditched like a brick'. I cited the story of the *Bermuda Queen*, a C class Empire flying boat of Imperial Airways. It put down in the Atlantic in an emergency situation and all on board were saved.

I am sure now that it was my cousins heavy involvement in equine matters and my enthusiastic description of our inspirational science teacher, Stan Ashby which turned things in my favour. My farewell party in the Mess was somewhat riotous. I was obliged to stay on for a day or so to clear up the mess in the Mess. In October of that year I walked into the Royal Veterinary College as a first year student entering the next phase of my life.

Our Short Sunderland flying boat PP 115 goes under Tower Bridge in
London during the Battle of Britain Week Celebrations in 1952

We moor up at Traitors Gate for the Tower of London. Our Captain
Fl Lt Simmons stands aloft. I pop my head out of a hatch nearby.

The 201 Squadron Christmas card picture in the 1950s

Myself in the driving seat of the Martin Mars water bomber in
Vancouver Island.

Chapter 3

Student Days

The Royal Veterinary College (RVC) in London is the oldest veterinary teaching establishment in the United Kingdom. It was the first veterinary school in the English speaking world. This was not the reason I applied for a place there. It was because it was in the South East of England and I would not have been able to afford to travel any farther from home. In the event it turned out to be exactly the right thing to do.

What I had seen as a serious setback, having failed one of my Higher School Certificate exams, proved to be very much to my advantage. The fact was that the RVC had just become part of the University of London, so we were studying for a Degree not just a Diploma. At the end of the course we would end up with both. They extended the final year to four terms resulting in the course lasting five and a half years. The hard part was getting through it all in that time. The good part was that we could enjoy the wonders of our field station where the Thames goes through the Chiltern Hills for our final four terms. This meant that we could indulge in periods of cricket, golf and messing about on the river, as well as the Streatley Revue and spending time and money in hostelries such as the Bull Inn. Then we had to get down to some very serious work in the last term. We were the very first of the BVetMed course, that is Bachelor of Veterinary Medicine students. In fact I think I was the very first to receive this qualification.

There were some sixty five students in our year, of whom only two were female. But Betty and Faith were splendid ladies. They coped well with what must have been a very intimidating situation at the time. The male to female balance has gone completely in the other direction now. It won't be long before the potential will be felt to the same level of a male minority as our girls put up with. It has been said that the present intake does not have enough players to make up a male rugby fifteen.

Our years were roughly divided into equal groups consisting of those straight from school and the rest, like myself having completed our National Service. The younger half treated studentship as an extension of the Sixth Form. Whereas, we who were all two years older tended to act as if we were still in uniform. The 'Young Ones' reminded us of the need to apply ourselves to learning and our ex-military types showed them how to have a good time. We came to believe that the combination of these two factors was what University Education was all about. It seemed to work anyway.

Another way the system differed in those days was that it was easier to get a place at the College than it is now, but much harder to survive the 'cut' of the exam tests. Nowadays students tend to be selected on their academic achievements so they are mostly very good at taking exams. There are advantages in both arrangements. The one prevailing in the 1950s took more notice of aptitude. The scheme now tends to recruit potential intellectual giants. You have to be a high flier in the IQ department to stand a chance of getting on the course. One big plus of the current system is that at least no-one asks 'why didn't you become a real doctor' any more. The 'chop rate' in earlier times was quite alarming as we progressed through the course, or didn't with many in our year. Some very high achievers in my profession failed some exams and were 'referred' en route. Sometimes this was for one term, others were put back one year. In the old days before the University course you could keep failing all the time as long as you paid your fees. In fact there were many left over from the old system who appeared to consider life at the College to be what they wanted to do in life, rather than go out into the wide world and try to earn a living. These were mostly students with parents who were comfortably off, some of whom were veterinarians seeking an heir to their business. This changed for us. We were allowed to fail only once. If you failed the resit, you were out. Of the sixty five of us, only fifteen got through the five and a half year course without any set backs. If anyone had told me this at the start, I would not have continued. If they had told me I would be one of the fifteen who made it to the end unscathed, I would not have believed them. But I was.

It must have presented considerable difficulties for the staff as it was the University curriculum they had to abide by. Just as it was at school, the quality of the tutors was very variable. Those who were good were very good. They cared about us and didn't just look on us as obstructions to their research programme. At the other end of the scale there were those who would have found it hard to get employment anywhere else. The individuals who motivated us were quite extraordinary. In our preclinical years before we got our hands on many live animals, we occupied ourselves with basic science in the form of physics, chemistry and zoology. Much of this had been covered in our sixth form days. In addition though we were taught animal husbandry and began to learn our anatomy and physiology in much the same way that those studying what I call 'ordinary medicine' did. The main difference was that we had a very wide range of species to tackle. One of the things that fascinates us who study animal medicine and surgery is that it covers horses, cattle, sheep, pigs, poultry ornamental fish even as well as companion animals such as dogs, cats, rabbits, cage birds, hamsters, gerbils and guinea pigs. Also, there are reptiles, llamas, zoo animals such as lions and tigers, ornamental and farmed fish. Above all though, in the eyes of the RVC in the 1950s, it was the horse, along with other Equidae, that predominated.

The elevation of the animal dissection specimen to a place in modern art would have surprised us then. We didn't know we were the precursors of the Damien Hirst school of the preservation of dead animals in formaldehyde. I suspect our unmade beds and unreliable lighting in our digs would have won us prizes if the modern art competitions had been on the lines of those of the present day.

Our Professors of Anatomy and of Physiology governed our lives during the early years of our studies. They were two most extraordinary individuals but they were complete opposites. They were clearly at war with each other. Everyone who was a student in my era has an 'Ammo' story. These relate to Professor Amoroso, Head of Physiology. He was one of the most striking people I have ever encountered. He had the greatest command of the English language of anyone I met before or since. His list of qualifications took up several lines in any professional record. He had a presence which no-one could avoid or resist. He had been a boxer at some stage in his career and wore a black patch on one eye. His bow tie would always become untied and droop from his substantial neck. He was originally from Trinidad and always looked as if he could have held his own against any of the Mike Tysons of his day. You never called him 'Ammo' in his presence, although we all knew him as that. I remember one idiot actually called him 'Snowball' to his face and we expected him to be torn apart. To our amazement our Professor fell about laughing. The only time he did in my experience. However, it was his first words to us that astonished me. He fixed me with his good eye and said in terrifying tones 'You will read your physiology **assiduously** or I will be **savage**'. I had never heard anyone speak like that before, not even when we were square bashing at RAF Padgate. We all read our physiology assiduously all right.

On the Anatomy side it was Professor Jimmy McCunn who ruled his area. He was one of the few veterinarians who had a medical qualification also. He was a very kind man. Not only did he encourage and inspire us, he was very generous as well. He would hand out the occasional reward for our efforts. Jimmy was a member of the MCC and would give us tickets for matches at Lords Cricket Ground when there was a Test Match or other game of interest on. He knew I played for the College XI and got me in to see Tests against Australia and South Africa. The one piece of generosity I will never forget was something completely different. Three of us, David Thornton, Bob Knowles and myself were walking down the corridor of the College having been working in the Dissection Room all morning. Professor McCunn came up to us and said that we had been working very hard lately and we could take the afternoon off (I have no knowledge of any other University staff saying anything on those lines). 'The BBC have given me these tickets for a recording at the Camden Theatre, so the three of you can go and relax there'. This venue is now a night club but it was a BBC Recording Studio at the time. It is also directly opposite Mornington Crescent Underground Station. A landmark which was to become a permanent joke in another BBC show.

We made our way to the Theatre and took our seats not knowing what the recording would be. It could have been a symphony concert or that weeks 'Come Dancing'. It was a bare stage with a set of microphones and a small table at the back for the sound effects man. We had a good position in the seats where we could see and hear exactly what was going on. On to the stage walked a team that was to become legendary in the next few years. We didn't know any of them at the time. They were Sid James, Bill Kerr, Kenneth Williams and the star of the show Tony Hancock. The lady who was to be replaced by the immortal Hattie Jacques, was Moira Lister. It turned out to be the very first 'Hancock's Half Hour'. A legend was born that day and we were there.

The cast went into their script with extraordinary skill. It was a completely different approach to comedy, their timing was as near to perfection as anyone could hope for. But about ten minutes into the recording the man in charge stopped everything. He apologised for the fact that one of the microphones was playing up and they would have to go back and start again. They did this straight away. The really amazing thing was they used the same words but timed it all quite differently. I have heard a recording of this particular show since. It is nothing like as good as many that followed but we still feel very privileged to have been there when it was born.

Most of us struggled to get past the first two pre-clinical exams but those who did entered clinical veterinary medicine at last. We saw real animals and studied pathology, the anatomy of disease that is; pharmacology the study of medicines; surgery that is surgical interference and internal medicine that is everything that can go wrong inside. I was even allowed to carry out an ovario-hysterectomy on a cat, that is it was my first spay. No-one can start with their second spay but at least this one was under close supervision. It survived and I was allowed to take the sutures out on my own. My next spay on my own was when I was in practice.

As we approached vacation time the most stressful part was waiting for the exam results. I could not afford to fail. One advantage I did have was a friend with close connections with the College administration. The coded message I would get by post if I was successful was that it was all right to get my cricket kit out as I would be playing in the summer term. Every time I worried as to whether this was correct or not, but it always was.

Vacation time was certainly not a holiday. For the first year I got no grant so my father had to pay all the fees. The Kent Education Committee considered his application for financial support for my second year. They agreed, provided I came up to scratch at the Kent Farm Institute where I was sent to work during the summer vacation. It was with the farm animals but in addition to feeding and cleaning out the pigs and attending to the sheep, I had to milk the cows at first light. They had quite a few dairy cows which were not suited to the milking machines of the time, so I had to milk them by hand. The Institute was some six miles up the North Downs and I had to get up at five o'clock every morning to cycle up there. At least it was down hill going home. This routine meant that nights out with the boys were out of the question, something for my parents to be pleased about. However, one Saturday there was a party I simply couldn't miss and I got home about four hours from the time I had to get up again. Even so I got to the milking parlour in time and sat down to get on with the milking. I sat on a stool and lent gently on the side of cow number one and went fast asleep. The cowman was not pleased to see my lack of progress.

The cowman was also the shepherd and the pigman. He then informed me that he was going on holiday the next day and he would leave me in charge. 'But how am I going to cope?' I said. ' We have to count all those lambs every day to make sure there are none missing'. 'I'll leave the dogs with you' was his reply. These were two beautiful Border Collies, Flanaghan and Allen. At least they knew what to do.

The pigs were easy. They just needed feeding and cleaning out more or less continuously. They were mostly friendly if you could keep up to speed with their nutritional requirements. I soon learned that a fully grown sow weighing more than 300 pounds could be formidable if upset. An entire boar could be really fearsome. But most of the time we got on well.

The seven rams were much more of a threat. If you entered the field they were in for whatever purpose, it was inevitable that you would have your back to at least one of them. The one thing that rams were good at was ramming you from behind. So you had to be very nimble on your feet to avoid serious damage. In the words of an Australian veterinarian 'sheep are deceptive in their ability to damage people'.

I wondered how I would go through the process of counting the 104 lambs we had in the lower field; but the dogs took me through it. They would get them in a tight bunch in one corner of the field. They would then drive them past at a rate which allowed me to count them accurately. Flanaghan would do the driving and Allen would control their speed by moving in closer if they were going too fast and and back away if they needed to go faster. The tricky part was when the critical mass of those that had been counted got large enough to make the remainder accelerate. The danger was that if they stopped, the first lot would try to go back from whence they came. After two weeks the little team of Flanaghan, Allen and Edney (in that order) became completely competent at sheep counting.

No matter how many lectures you attend or publications you read, although they are a real help, getting skilled at animal handling has to be done hands on in the field. One of the many tips I picked up at the Farm Institute was to be very careful of the last cow in the shed. They had a habit of leaning on you if you got between half a ton of cow and an unyielding wall.

It was back to the College for year two as I had scraped over the first major exam hurdle. Kent County Education Committee allowed a modest grant to ease the financial burden on my parents.

I had heard about the horrible fogs which occupied the capital most years but I wasn't prepared for my first one. That winter was to see the worst London Smog of the century. Some of my colleagues officiated at the Smithfield Agricultural Show at Earls Court. They took a plentiful supply of whisky with them, allegedly to dose the suffering cattle but most finished up fortifying the veterinary staff. The very heavy fog was quite unpleasant for us to breathe throughout central London. It even got down into the underground stations so the tube trains were held up. Even inside The Royal Veterinary College it was difficult to see across the main hall. Once it had cleared, the wreckage resulting from vehicles driving into shop windows was appalling. Although the clean air legislation changed all this, another foggy experience stays with me. Several years later I was trying to navigate my way along a main road in Surrey in my new car as the fog thickened. So much so that I had to open the side window and drive along what I thought was the white line in the middle of the road. I realised that it was actually the pavement on the other side of the road just in time to avoid a catastrophe.

There were many interesting characters amongst my fellow students. There are many in my profession who would be prime candidates for the 'Flawed Geniuses Club'. One stands out as quite extraordinary. Brian Nettleton was a true eccentric. He was always known as 'Nettleton' and he became something of a celebrity without knowing it. He had the ability to fail examinations beyond the limit normally allowed and still continue. Every time he failed his Pharmacology he would go round the College corridors dressed in a kilt playing a dirge on his accordion. When we heard this sound during our lectures we just assumed Nettleton had failed his Pharmacology again. Shortly after these episodes we all ceased work for the day as a film was being shot in Camden Town which was to become a classic. It was a remake of the Alfred Hitchcock drama 'The Man Who Knew Too Much'. The great man was there, with James Stewart and a sizeable film crew. The reason they were there was that there was a taxidermist's studio nearby which was to feature in the story.

They filmed Mr Stewart riding in a taxi up Royal College Street, stopping, getting out and walking up Plender Street in Camden Town. Whilst this took all day, it lasts about a minute in the film. All this was too good an opportunity for Nettleton to resist. He put on a smart striped blazer, wore a colourful cravat and a Panama hat. He walked along the street close to Hitchcock and got several of his friends to come over and ask him for his autograph. The locals immediately thought he was part of the Hollywood set and besieged him with anything they could find for him to sign. What they have in their autograph books and what they make of it now we can only guess. It was a perfect jape and characteristic of Nettleton, in that it was original, hilarious and harmed no-one. Which is more than you can say about some of the pranks we got up to.

When Nettleton finally made it to his final year at the College Field Station which was then at Streatley on Thames he came across a litter of orphan badgers. He reared them to adulthood and wrote a paper on his technique for a professional journal. He took them everywhere with him on leads like a litter of Dachshunds, which invited a good deal of comment. He even went for his job interview with them to Yorkshire. It was none other than the great James Alfred Wight's practice in Thirsk. Alf Wight is better known as the most famous veterinarian in the world, one James Herriot. Alf told me about his first encounter with Nettleton when we met in the Golden Fleece hostelry in Thirsk, Darrowby in the Herriot books. He calls him Callum Buchanan in the Herriot stories. In life he sat before his potential boss for the job interview for the position of assistant in the practice. Alf was struck dumb at first sight of his applicant. Nettleton began asking questions about the salary he could expect and if a car was part of the deal, time off and so on. 'What's that on your shoulder? asked Alf. 'Oh it's a badger' replied Nettleton as if it was perfectly normal for someone to come for a job interview so arrayed. He got the job and performed very well in the mixed practice. He eventually went off to Nova Scotia for a while but decided it was too cold and wet there and moved off to New Guinea where he found it to be too hot and humid. He returned to Canada but tragically he was killed in a car crash. Alf Wight wrote a touching obituary saying that 'for all his eccentricities, he was a very good vet'. This was all the farmers cared about. He said they would ring up and ask for the 'vet wit badgers' to call.

The clinical years put us in another gear. Although the work rate became frantic immersing us in Pathology, Surgery and clinical disease recognition, treatment and prevention, meat inspection and many related subjects. Even so all this did not prevent a high level of extra-mural activity, and not just in the pubs. We played cricket, hockey, rugby and badminton for the College. Every term saw a production by the RVC Theatre Group. Of the three plays we put on each year for the first four years 'Home and Beauty', 'On Monday Next', 'An Inspector Calls' and 'The Lady's Not for Burning' stand out in my memory. I helped build the set and paint the scenery. I had a part in some of them. The Christopher Fry work had me playing Mathew Skipps a drunken rag and bone man. I was either Burke or Hare, I can't remember which in 'The Anatomist' by James Bridie which I directed. We even had a real anatomist as the lead. It would be wonderful to see these productions again to check that they really were as good as we thought they were. The tradition of The Final Year Revue was maintained but we broke new ground in that our satirising of the College world was the first in living memory that was not obscene (in our opinion).

Living in digs away from the College had its advantages as we mixed with students from many other disciplines. Socialising with many studying medicine, dentistry, law and other professions broadened our mind. London in the 1950s had a rich seam of culture especially theatrical art. In particular we could go to the Old Vic theatre for a few pence to see legends such as Ralph Richardson, John Gielgud and most memorably, Richard Burton. Burton's stage presence was electrifying. Even in relatively small parts you were always waiting for him to come on stage, no matter what else was going on. Subsequent live performances of Henry V and Sir Toby Belch in Twelfth Night will always be compared with his in my memory. For a short period Burton shared the parts of Othello and Iago with John Neville. We queued for Gallery tickets for one shilling and sixpence. Farther forward and it would have cost us half a crown, nearly twice the price of the seats at the back. We sat in the back two rows of the 'Gods' in the belief that Burton would be playing the lead. In the event it was Neville who was Othello that evening. But as soon as Richard came on we realised that he ran the show and the play should have been called Iago.

As the final years approached with the vital exams which could steer us into the career we were aiming for, work got very serious indeed. We still had our fun but had to bury our heads in text books and lecture notes for hours on end. The extensive memory I had at the time served me well. I had drawn caricatures of the lecturers in the margins of my notes which helped to recall large sections at exam time. All my spare time during the day was spent in the Library Annex. So much so that I was known as 'Annex Edney' at the time.

Pranks were eventually put behind us as we prepared for a professional life. Our last two ventures into prank land disappeared into history. I can only hope that those on the receiving end have put it down to the process of growing up.

The College had bought Hawkshead Farm near Potters Bar just North of London. This was to become the permanent 'Field Station' and later the 'Queen Mother Hospital' and the 'Sefton Equine Hospital'. We were supposed to have been the first students to use the facility but we were not even the last ones to go to Streatley on Thames. The new site had a large notice stating that it had been 'Sold to the Royal Veterinary College'. The pranksters in our year (not me this time) removed it and attached it to the Craven A Cigarette Factory in Camden Town. By chance the matter was reported in the papers immediately before a strike of journalists. So the story remained on the tables of readers around the country for a week longer than it should have.

We were at the College when the candidates for a place were being interviewed. As they emerged from their ordeal we directed them towards the 'second interview room'. This was actually the Students' Common Room but it was set out as room to interrogate hopeful students. What made it credible was that the 'Chairman' was Henry Merlen, our anatomist who had been one of the genuine interviewers. He wasn't above a lark or two. Henry would ask if the candidate had done Latin at school. If they said they had not he would press them to make up the deficit 'as some of the lectures are in Latin'. We did the right thing at the end of each interview. We explained that it had all been a joke and would not effect their future prospects as they had had the real thing earlier. There was one exception though. We did not take to the last person we interviewed and told him we were undecided and asked him to sit in the corridor to await further interrogation. Then we went home. Fortunately he did not have to wait there long. The College Bursar passed by and asked what he was doing there. 'I'm waiting for my third interview' was his reply, and that was the end of that.

In our final year we exchanged the metropolitan ambiance of London for the beautiful surroundings of the Chiltern Hills. It was 'Three Men in a Boat' country. We made the most of our last days in Camden Town as there seemed to be an outbreak of pretty wild nights out after our fourth year exams. This must have been clearly evident when I got home. Mother asked me 'What time did you go to bed last night?'. I said 'Thursday' which was not well received by either parent. I was told in no uncertain fashion that I was there to work hard not to enjoy myself. They did not entertain the idea that it was possible to do both, which we did. It was our concept of a University Education.

The final year field station was located where the river Thames goes through the Chiltern Hills. The University had added a term. We thought that this was somewhat tedious at first. However, we soon learned that we were able to enjoy an idyllic summer fitting work in where we could. We had free use of the local Golf Club, played cricket and borrowed a skiff from the local pub to row up the river. The fact that we rowed up to the next pub did not seem to bother the very generous landlord of the Leathern Bottle.

Our final term in the winter was very different. We all worked relentlessly to catch up. The summer term had ended with our famous but very amusing non-obscene Final Year Revue which we managed to fit in. It was well on into the riotous party after this event that we realised we had the traditional last cricket match the next day. After very little sleep we had to take on the combined forces of the two local clubs. It was the first time in my career I opened the batting for the College; and we destroyed them! I still have a copy of the scorecard.

'Seeing practice' with veterinary surgeons was in earnest during vacations. It's called 'Extra-mural Studies' now. I have several very busy professionals to thank for giving freely of their time and drew on their extensive experience. Previously I had mostly been given the task of opening and closing farm gates. As I progressed in my studies I got much nearer cases and was even allowed to do some minor surgery, under strict supervision of course. You never stop learning. It was my first encounter with the 'while you're here' request. This usually turned out to be something the client hadn't the nerve to tell you about when requesting a visit. It wasn't so much that you had gone to dress a cat's ears, something you had anticipated would not take long. It was the several Wildebeest in the back field that you had to castrate that had 'got left'. The additional job would invariably take longer than you had allowed, so upsetting your timetable for the day. Speak to plumbers, carpenters, electricians and the like and they will sympathise.

One veterinarian I saw practice with was plunged out of his depth when he was asked 'and while you're here can you please sex the parrot?' He knew it was an African Grey but not much else. He took a rather superficial look and said confidently 'it's a female'. I was impressed. As we drove off I asked how he knew it was female. His reply was that 'he didn't know, but if it lays an egg we'll be covered.' True I thought, but I will have to do better than that.

All this seemed a long way from the lectures, swotting and exams. But exams had to be endured and they had to be passed somehow. In common with most degree courses this took many hours of preparation and colossal feats of memory. Although it was easier to gain a place at any of the British Veterinary Schools at this time, the 'chop rate' could be severe. After five and a half years of scrambling over all these hurdles, it was time to face three days of three hour written exams. Although I was better at writing than speaking, I occasionally came across words I had never seen before. All this was very unnerving. But it was the *viva voce*, that is the oral tests which very nearly threw me. My brain would rapidly assume a jellylike constituency. This began when, somewhat unusually I turned up in good time for my place in the alphabetical order only to find the 'Bs' were still being processed. It was some two hours before it was the turn of the 'Es'. I had that time to sit there without any papers going through a mental list of things I knew very little about hoping I was not asked anything about them. I was subsequently savaged at length by one examiner in Surgery. So much so that the other examiner present didn't get a word in and eventually walked out. The Medicine viva almost came as a relief.

When it was all over we sat with our battered brains in The Bull Hotel, a local hostelry attempting to ease our anxieties with generous doses of fine ale. My contact who had always let me know how I had been adjudged had fallen by the wayside. In any case his code message to 'get my cricket kit out for the coming season' would not have had the same interpretation as in previous years. In fact it would have had the opposite meaning. By chance I spotted a member of the College staff sitting in a quiet corner of the bar. As I had played in the local cricket side with him it was at least worth asking if I had passed. It was 'Poppa' Lewis a well rounded, avuncular South African who I put in a difficult position. He came over all serious and declined my offer of another beer. Predictably he said that he was frequently asked this question and to let on who had passed wouldn't be fair on those who hadn't. There were several failures, but he told me 'not to worry as I wasn't one of them'!

It wasn't until I was invited to the Royal Albert Hall for the graduation ceremony that I really took in that I was at last to be a veterinary surgeon. We were given a choice of two dates to attend this occasion. In the event I was to be the alphabetically first in line for the earlier date. As it was a new degree I believe I was the very first Bachelor of Veterinary Medicine of the University of London. Unfortunately they did not have enough of the BVetMed hoods for my academic gown. Queen Elizabeth the Queen Mother who made the presentations did not mention this omission. I made up for it some forty years later by wearing the full regalia when I became a Doctor of Veterinary Medicine of the University of London, DVetMed.

However, in January 1958 I still had to be admitted to The Royal College of Veterinary Surgeons. So at an equally memorable event I signed the RCVS Register on making the traditional Declaration. This required us all to agree *inter alia* that our constant endeavour would for the welfare of the 'animals in our care'. At last I had a degree and a diploma and was a real vet.

The Royal Veterinary College Cricket Club Team in 1956, myself
seated far right

Opening batsmen Andrew Edney left, Mike Griffin right for the
annual match against Streatley on Thames Cricket Club in 1957

The RVC Theatre Group production of 'The Anatomist' by James
Bridie with body snatchers David Thornton as Burke and Andrew Edney
as Hare

In the play 'The Anatomist' the anatomist Dr Knox was played by an
anatomist, Henry Merlen

The RVC Year of '58 on the Magdalen Barge at The Swan Hotel
Streatley on Thames for our big reunion in 2008

Receiving an Open University Masters Degree in History at The
Royal Festival Hall in London in the year 2000

THE ROYAL VETERINARY COLLEGE

Receiving my Doctorate in Veterinary Medicine at The Royal
Veterinary College in 1998

Chapter 4

Practice

It is easy to deceive oneself on graduation that you have somehow taken on special powers on the day your life changes. In fact your skills are not going to be very different for some time. In our case we suddenly became employable as there was a shortage of veterinarians. Up to that point my means of earning a living had been restricted to farm labouring and military service.

As I, along with most of my classmates had elected to go into general practice, there was a need to have a licence to drive a motor vehicle. I was very pleased to be offered a job in deepest Hampshire, the county of my paternal ancestors, even though I had to confess that I had yet to take my driving test. The principal of the practice seemed surprisingly relaxed about this shortcoming. He said 'Don't worry, my wife will drive you around until you pass'.

My driving instructor Ray was determined that I would get through my test. He went out of his way to spend time on giving me a good deal of information on how they went about the test. He took me to Canterbury and showed me the route I would be taking, pointing out where they would try to catch me turning into a badly signed 'no-entry'. He identified the spot where they invariably called the emergency stop and where I would be doing the three point turn. Even so, there were clearly still some shortcomings in my performance but I put on the look of sheer determination that Ray was sure would be effective in the circumstances; and it was. The examiner in the seat beside me eventually said 'Well, I'll give you a pass', in distinctly patronising tones. But that was all I wanted and off I went to pick up my very first car. It was a rather aged Standard 8 which went with the job. It had no extras such as heating or radio set, apart from the in-car radio telephone. It was a mobile phone in the sense that it went round with me as it was part of the fixtures on the dashboard. Still it was my first car and the practice paid for the petrol and servicing. Ray emigrated to Australia.

Everyone remembers their first car. Two things remain in my memory about the dear old Standard. The boss's car was out of action for a couple of days. He gave me all the operations to carry out in the surgery while he sped around the countryside in my motor. Vets are not noted for keeping their motor transport neat and tidy, especially when engaged in farm work. I was however told off for the strong smell which could be picked up from well outside the car. I soon realised that a black bag had been left in the boot when the vehicle was returned to me. It contained a dead cat which should have been interred several days before. A vigorous clean-up and respectful burial put matters right.

The other fault the car had was a reluctance to start from cold, a trait shared with myself. I ran a local cricket team, this being the only way I could be sure of getting a game at a reasonable level. This did allow me to make some very good friends. One acquaintance ran a garage just down the road. When we met in the local pub I mentioned the vehicles reluctance to start. 'Oh bring it in any time' he said, so I did. He sat in the driving seat and pressed the starter button a number of times. There was no response at all but he persisted. 'Mike' I said as politely as I could 'you have to switch the ignition on first'. He did not have to deal with such mundane matters in his real job. 'You try driving one of my racing cars and see how you get on' was his reply. For he was none other than Mike Hawthorn. He was World Motor Racing Champion at the time, the equivalent of Formula 1 today. Very tragically Mike was killed when his prototype of the E-Type Jaguar left the road on the Guildford Bypass the following year. Every time I drive past the tree he collided with I wish he rests in peace.

So, I had my car with a boot full of all the usual medicaments and tools for the job as well as my little black bag to carry around. But, I had all the theory but very little of the practical experience to be what is called 'omnicompetent'. That is you are expected to deal with every species that moved that wasn't human. Even then I have had the odd request to deal with people. It took me about eight years to get really good at all the veterinary work.

My first task in practice was to do the evening surgery at the local RSPCA Clinic. My very first patient was a tortoise. It had an accumulation of mucus on its tongue. This was not too difficult to remove. I awaited my next case. A lady walked in with a cardboard box. One is always a little apprehensive when such containers were held by clients sitting in the waiting room. They usually have in them what the Americans call 'parcel pets' and they can be just about anything. This time the lady put the box on the table and opened it to reveal **two** tortoises. For a moment I had this disturbing vision of an arithmetic progression of ever increasing tortoises. Fortunately it was several days before I encountered another Chelonian.

It is the enormous variety of cases one is called upon to deal with that makes veterinary medicine so rewarding if more than a little demanding. It is true that much of the time you are neutering, vaccinating and doing other tasks which do not require five and a half years of University tuition. However, it is drummed into you from an early stage of training that you need to examine carefully even the most routine case. This way you can spot early tumours, dental deposits, parasites, eye problems and many other conditions at an early stage and deal with them effectively. It is worth comparing the need for highly developed skills with those of an airline pilot. Flying an aircraft is relatively easy. Getting it up in the air is a result of making it go faster and pointing it upwards. Landing is a touch more tricky but the part in between one leaves mostly to George, the automatic pilot. It is when something goes wrong that all that training pays dividends in what can be life and death situations. One such case was presented to our practice. It appeared to be a complete mystery. The dog did not want to eat although it had a history of being quite greedy. Two veterinary surgeons had seen it and prescribed numerous medicines. Another had removed small amounts of dental deposit and dealt with mild inflammation of the gums. None of these procedures had made any difference at all. It was a large dog being a cross between a Dobermann and some other sizeable breed. Fortunately it was not too difficult to handle. It allowed me to do a thorough examination during which I noticed something unusual. It had what appeared to be a stripe across the roof of its mouth. This stretched across the widest part of the palate. At some risk to my fingers and with some difficulty I managed to get some movement in what appeared to be a foreign object. It turned out to be the remains of a stick which had been buried in the palate. The dog having crushed the stick had left a length wedged across the roof of its mouth. Granulation had covered this object so that it was all but hidden from view. Even though the area remained inflamed for several days after we had removed the piece of wood, the dog's appetite returned right away. It also cheered up no end, as did its owner.

My first calving on my own was at the estate of a prominent peer of the realm. His Lordship was present and along with his cowman took his turn at the ropes which I had attached to the calf which remained obstinately *in utero*. I knew I had aligned the calf in the correct position to enter this world but it didn't do so. I have to say that I got into a mild panic, which was in danger of becoming one of full sized proportions. I had allowed a short period for this visit and we were already well into extra time. So, I went out to the car and telephoned the boss of the practice. He reassured me that he would be on his way immediately, although it was his day off. However, when I got back into the cow shed, the new calf, an Aberdeen Angus was walking around in the best of health. I learned from this to give calvings time.

The next day the boss had another 'emergency'. He had an urgent call to go to a truck which was on fire about twenty miles away. It was said to be full of horses. It is easy to imagine the very mixed thoughts that went through his mind as he drove furiously along a very busy trunk road to get to the site. When he got there he found the truck which was still burning. However, the 'horses' where part of a carousel in transit with all the fairground equipment.

My experience with equine dramas is mostly less bizarre. On one occasion I was on duty on a Bank Holiday Sunday. I was required to go to a horse in a field for a 'very urgent matter'. That was all the information I had apart from the location of the animal. It was on the other side of the practice which meant that I had to go as fast as I could across some 35 miles of countryside. I got to the horse in a field when I should have been sitting down to Sunday lunch. The horse showed signs of ringworm, a fungal infection hardly an emergency. When I questioned the owner as to why he didn't contact us earlier or at least left it another 24 hours, his reply was curt to say the least. 'Oh I couldn't do that' he said 'I run a riding establishment and I don't want it to get around that my horses have ringworm'.

Some years later I had a real equine drama. It was a road accident on a busy London Road. A child had ridden her horse down a narrow bridle path and across the main road as if it wasn't there. A very large truck had no chance of stopping and sent them all flying. A nearby resident had telephoned every veterinary practice in the Yellow Pages, including ours. As I had the fastest car, an MGB and used to drive like Fangio in those days, I got there first and fought my way through the many bystanders to the horse now lying injured in the gardens of a nearby property. The problem with such accident cases is usually that there are often masses of people in various states of hysteria getting in the way and shouting conflicting advice as to what should or should not be done. The first move in these situations is to get rid of everyone not directly involved. The truck driver was the most manic of those remaining. He thought he had killed the child and the horse. The child, although injured was demented about the possible loss of her trusty equine companion. We got her into a bedroom in a bungalow nearby and tried to settle her down with reassurances. I was very foolish to tell her that 'her horse would be all right'. I soon realised that this was not a sensible thing to say as there was a good chance that I would be proved wrong. You can give a guarded prognosis but never risk a definite promise. This can apply both ways. It is bad enough if you say it will get better and it doesn't. If for example you say a young dog with a tumour will die in six months and it is best to end its life and the owner does not comply, it is not impossible that they go elsewhere and it lives another twelve years. They will not be shy about telling everyone they know how wrong you were. In this case the animal had broken its jaw. This was repaired by a colleague who was hot stuff in this area of surgery. So, I was spared and so was the horse. Mercifully it was reunited with the young child and she was happy. I don't know what happened to the truck driver.

One of the differences between veterinary medicine and what I call 'ordinary medicine' is that ours is a three cornered relationship. Animal patients have owners who need to be questioned and advised. At the same time I have to examine the animal and treat it. A comparable situation in human medicine is in paediatrics, where the 'owner' is usually the parent. One advantage that we have though is that our patients tend not to malinger, although they may well exhibit marked attention getting behaviour. One such dog of mixed ancestry was called 'Spenser'. I asked if he had any connection with the poet Edmund Spenser who wrote 'The Fairie Queene' as he was spelled in that way. The owner was quick to reply that it was because he had a brother called 'Mark'. Spenser appeared to have a serious problem with his right foreleg giving him the appearance of marked lameness. However, a thorough examination failed to reveal any abnormality. My suspicions were aroused when he took on an entirely different view of life when his owner left the room for a few minutes. This prompted me to ask her to let him out into her extensive but safely enclosed garden at the rear of the house. We watched from indoors as Spenser limped pathetically while his owner was in sight. As soon as he was on his own though he went round the garden like a deer chased by a lion. Naturally he immediately went back to the 'my poor front leg is giving me a lot of pain' mode as soon as he got back indoors. A behavioural rehabilitation regime was implemented. As soon as Spenser realised that if he tried it on again he would be ignored, he got back to normal quite rapidly. The trick was to give him the attention he craved when he did the right thing rather than punishing him for misbehaving.

Every companion animal veterinary practice has its share of eccentric clientele. Some can be amusing, others usually a very small minority, can be very unreasonable. They can get you out in the middle of the night for an animal that has been ill for days, or because they have insomnia. One such insisted that I call to carry out the regular examination of the anal sacs of their rather bad tempered Pekingese. My orders were that 'I must be there before ten o'clock' as they were going to church. It was Christmas Day.

There is always someone who never seems to know when to stop taking more animals into their home. One such was a Mrs O'Malley. She bred toy dogs by the boat load. They all had a wonderful temperament but were full of mange mites. They lived in excessive squalor. Mrs O'M seemed incapable of implementing any of the treatment regimes I advised or even basic standards of hygiene. When clients came in with dogs they had got from this source I could tell immediately where they had come from. There were also quite a few cats running loose in the house. They would do a wall of death circuit around the room on my arrival and would occasionally disappear up the chimney. One such event occurred one morning. All the cats rushed out of the front door as the lady of the house opened it. She then said in a loud voice 'Now look what you've done, you've let them all out'. On leaving I requested an opportunity to wash my hands. Her reply was 'Yes, you can use that towel, it is dirty'.

It is easy to get hung up on the more weird owners and forget that the great majority are charming, cooperative and friendly. I wasn't ready for an encounter with one family on one of my early house calls. No-one had told me they were nudists and I found it difficult to concentrate on the animals.

There were a number of indicators I soon learned to beware of. When I started out in practice I was enraptured by a client who gave me the highest praise after only a few consultations. She also rubbished every other veterinarian in the locality. It wasn't long though that I was on the end of her severe criticism. This became a little more bearable when I discovered that all those who followed me suffered the same tirades. The other clear indicator of potential trouble was the phrase ' I don't mind how much it costs'. It didn't need a high IQ to work out why; they weren't going to pay us'.

A couple of dog breeders brought their Miniature Dachshunds into our evening surgery and were more than I little sniffy as they whined 'Oh you're not Mr . . . 'the veterinary surgeon they were used to seeing. The problem was not unusual as the person on duty always did the evening stint. So they could well see someone different on several occasions if they could only get to the later opening times. In the event we later became good friends and I still get Christmas cards every year. I eventually asked why they had been so stand-offish. The lady of the pair said that they had got fed up with seeing a different person each time they came in, and then to be confronted with a vet who looked little more than a schoolboy'. I discovered later that she was only two years older than me.

More amusing were clients who gave their animals funny names. A local vicar had a cat called 'Magnificat' and a classics teacher with one called 'Oedipuss'. He also kept a hen named 'Menelaus'. Rather more embarrassing was when I was filling in a new clients particulars on the cards we used at the time. 'Name?' I asked. 'Joker' the lady said. 'No I want your name not the dog's.' It **is** my name' she replied.

The variety of size and shape of dogs is unequalled in any other mammalian species. When puppies come in for their first vaccination it can be difficult to determine the breed and even more to determine the origins when they are crossbred individuals. One such was a very strange looking dog. So much so that the owner volunteered information about its ancestry without me having to ask. 'It's a cross between a Standard Poodle and a Miniature Dachshund; and it happened on the stairs'. I didn't enquire which way round this liaison had taken place.

Our surgery was in town where I was the only practising veterinary surgeon dealing with every kind of animal. As my career developed the percentage of veterinary work with companion animals increased steadily to the point where it now represents well over 70% of all such work carried out in the United Kingdom. So I moved away from mixed practice to dealing mainly with pets at about the right time. This still included the occasional equine patient. One such arrived at my surgery in the middle of town. We were on the first floor over a butcher's shop. This did not strike me as at all strange until I got a letter addressed to 'The vet over the butchers in Union Street'. There were two other businesses in the same building. They were an insurance agent and a ladies hairdressers.

The patient was a pony which was the mascot of a regiment from the military base nearby. Two military gentlemen arrived in some distress. One held the pony on the busy street below. The other knocked on the consulting room door. We sat him down and asked him just to tell us what the problem was. He explained that they had been applying blanco to their kit in preparation for a major parade. A large splash of the white stuff had gone down the animal's near side. I said I did not think that this was life threatening and with some vigorous washing and some careful clipping all would eventually be well. He said that they were well aware of this but they were all due to go on parade within the hour. Serious disciplinary action would certainly follow if we didn't make the stains disappear. After a few moments of desperate thought I came up with an idea. On the next floor up was the ladies hairdressers establishment run by a pair of brothers. They proved to be our saviour. Their skilful application of a hair-dye which was a close match for the Bay pony did the trick. The parade with the mascot went ahead without any repercussions.

Further involvement with the armed forces occurred quite often. The delightful Audrey who ran the practice office sent me off to see a dog at a pub in town. She said it was 'The Circling Camel'. I had a fairly good knowledge of the local licensed premises, this was not just for their social benefits but they were good navigation points. I had never heard of this one. After an extended search the place I sought turned out to be the 'Sir Colin Campbell'. This was a pub named after the military hero of Lucknow in 1857. It had no connection with desert animals.

One of my clients worked for the Aircraft Establishment at Farnborough. He asked me to call at his place of work. I turned up at the main gate expecting to be asked for details of the reason for my visit. To my surprise the uniformed heavies on duty waved me in without even stopping me. As I was early and had an interest in aviation, I decided to do a brief tour of the facility as it was only a few days away from the great air show. My client was more than a little annoyed that I had not been checked as he was the Officer in Charge of Security there.

My Air Force connections eventually resulted in my having free access to the Empire Test Pilots School Mess. This brought back memories of the lively life I had experienced in the Mess at RAF Pembroke Dock. One night in the bar in Farnborough I couldn't help noticing an RAF Officer who had gone rather too far in pursuit of social enjoyment. This was because he was lying semiconscious on the floor of the mess. No-one seemed at all concerned about him. I was told that this was par for the course for this particular officer. Further enquiries revealed that he was to lead the Aerobatic Team which was to perform the next day at the air show. The following day he was up there with his squadron giving a faultless display aloft.

As time passed I graduated to a large vehicle to drive around the practice. It was an Austin 16 which had a sizeable radio aerial on the roof as we had a radio telephone on board. It looked very much like one of the local taxis. In the Mess during the Farnborough Air Show I left well before midnight, which was unusual. As I left a group of five or six German visitors decided to depart at the same time. To my surprise they all got into my car just as I was about to depart. Their grasp of English was marginally better than my German, making discussion somewhat restricted. 'Ve are vanting the George Hotel' one said. Clearly they thought I was the taxi service. My feeling was that it might be quicker to ferry them to the hotel than to try to explain that I was the local tierarzt. The trouble was that there were several George Hotels in the locality. 'Which George do you want? I enquired. 'The pub hotel' was all they came up with. So for the next hour or so we had a tour of the countryside ticking off all the George Hotels in the area. Whether the fifth one was actually the one they were booked in, I don't know but they all got out there. When I said there was nothing to pay their look of astonishment would have been marvellous to record. It was worth the trouble I had taken to see their reaction. I wonder what their story was when they got back home.

One of the joys of veterinary practice is that it is seldom boring. You never know what is going to turn up next. The drawback though is that it can be very demanding. Of these situations cruelty cases can be very vexatious. The role of the expert witness puts one in a very vulnerable position. You are very much on the legal people's ground. Fortunately the few occasions I have appeared in court in this role have not resulted in me being taken apart.

One cruelty case sticks in my memory. It was unusual in that it had a happy ending. The subject was a Miniature Poodle. He was known as Doodle the Poodle. Doodle lived in a multi-dog household where he was bottom of the canine hierarchy. Some youths, who were subsequently dealt with by the courts, had abused the animal and thrown him into a quarry. He broke both his front legs. Our job was to repair them as soon as we could. This was long before the present elaborate fixation techniques had become commonplace. We put substantial plaster casts on his front legs. Doodle then looked rather like a toy soldier carrying two heavy rifles.

Our patient soon became accustomed to these impediments. He was walking quite well in a few days. Then he rapidly learned that he could adjust his position in the pecking order by giving his house mates a good clout with one and then the other plastered leg. After a few weeks he had clouted his way to become master of the household canine population. Then the time came for the plasters to come off. You could see that Doodle was very disappointed with this. However, he was too clever to be pushed back to his position as the lowest member of the household. After a few more days he learned that he did not actually have to hit the other dogs to maintain his supremacy. He only had to make threatening gestures as if he was still plastered. He never looked back.

Whilst the Doodle story had a happy ending, an experience with a fearsome dog resulted in a last minute escape. Most of the town where I practised was respectable, well behaved, crime free and in some parts slightly boring. However, there was a small area to the North East which you only visited if you had to. It was said that 'the Alsatians went round in pairs' there. It was here that I learned one of the most chilling lessons of my career.

The dog I visited at regular intervals was a mainly German Shepherd Dog with a number of genes from individuals of varying degrees of unpleasantness. He had not had a kindly upbringing and was one of those animals that 'did not like men'. In his three years of existence he had not benefited from any appreciable level of socialisation with man or beast. He especially did not like vets who came up to his fourth floor apartment to inspect his, smelly ears and anal glands. Worst of all this dog's owner was not the alpha individual on the territory she occupied with this disagreeable GSD.

Having done my best to examine the dog and to apply various medications to the inflamed areas of his body after our regular struggle, his owner uttered words which sounded quite decisive. From across the other side of the room she bellowed 'I'm fed up with all this, I want **it** put to sleep'. I knew it would be fruitless countering this by suggesting dog training classes or any other form of schooling. So I opened my black bag, took out a large syringe and filled it with the concentrated barbiturate solution we used to dispatch animals on their last journey. That is it induced anaesthesia beyond the point of no return.

I managed to secure the biting regions with my trusty pyjama cord, forming a muzzle. Using a modified wrestling manoevre I was ready to inject. Just as I was on the point of ending this dog's life, the owner casually asked when I would be along again for his usual check-up. 'But you said . . . . !' I began to stutter until I realised that she wanted me to anaesthetise her dog and not to kill him. The lesson I learned from all this was that where euphemisms for killing are used you need to be absolutely sure that is what is required. Nowadays it is usual to get a consent form signed and to discuss what was going to happen afterwards regarding the disposal of the body. All this happened towards the end of my spell in general practice so I never found out if this dog lived for maybe ten years. But I doubt it.

Life in practice was not all harrowing experiences, although we had our share. There were many happy memories. It is always a joy to see an animal you have treated walking happily down the street when you know that its healthy state is a result of your intervention. A couple of successes are a pleasure to recall. A West Highland White Terrier was brought in to the surgery in considerable pain. It was trying to vomit but was unproductive. A radiograph showed a large piece of a bone stuck in the oesophagus where it enters the stomach. We did not have the equipment to carry out intra-thoracic surgery and I certainly did not have the necessary skills for such a procedure at that stage of my career. There was no time to seek the help of those who had. So I excavated the fragment from the stomach upwards. It was a tricky job to sew it all up again. In the event the dog made a remarkably rapid recovery. What really cheered me up was the apparent gratitude the little Westie showed me afterwards. I would like to think he knew I had saved his life.

Another drama came soon afterwards with another client who bred Spaniels. Two of them lay unconscious near to death on the floor of the kitchen of their splendid house in the upmarket local rural area. A third dog looked distinctly wobbly nearby. My first thought was that it could have been something they had eaten. I then started to feel a little unstable myself. Fortunately I then spotted a very large cooker which seemed to be malfunctioning across the room. This made me think of Carbon Monoxide toxicity. Sure enough, taking all the dogs outside into the well ventilated garden area they all returned to normal. CO being heavier than air had occupied the space down at dog level. It could have eventually resulted in death of the whole family in an enclosed space. I left the clients the task of sorting the cooker out.

Life was not all stressful cases stretching my abilities to the limit. Time off allowed some indulgence in non-veterinary activities. We were a four man practice which meant that each of us had to do one night on in four, seven days a week. This meant that the duty vet covered the whole practice after hours. Even so the boss or his wife took all the calls and allocated them accordingly. Cricket and motor rally driving took up much of my time off. That is in addition to what my friends called 'in pursuance of the act'. With a hope that it would avoid any *in vivo* fertilisation. That subject could fill a whole book.

I still have a reputation for having wrecked a few cars. I fact I only wrote off one but went close to doing the same to myself. We will enlarge on this incident shortly. The motor sport we indulged in took the form of navigation rallies, mostly on public roads at night. We won a few trophies and competed as 'experts' for several years. This required some driving skill but it relied very much on the abilities of my navigator Brian. His mastery of the Ordnance Survey maps was unparalleled. The only serious mishap occurred when we tried to negotiate a back lane which was flooded. We had been warned but we thought that if we could make it through we would have a time advantage over the other competitors. We came to a halt in the middle of it. 'You'll have to get out and push' said Brian, 'You've got the Wellington Boots'. I had indeed but the water came well over the top of these. So we both had to push the car for what seemed like a couple of miles but was probably a few hundred yards. Later an opportunity did arise to drive a sports car around the Silverstone motor race track but my tonsils got the better of me and I had to go into hospital to have them removed.

A great highlight of my cricketing efforts came when the Lords Taverners team came to our village. England fast bowler Tyson, Frank not Mike that is, bowled so quickly I didn't actually see the ball going down the pitch. But it was the stars of radio and television who made it thrilling just to be in their presence. Of these Harry

Secombe, Eric Sykes stand out along with the immortal Tony Hancock. I stood with Sykes in the Barley Mow pub after the match. We chatted away as he picked up my lady friend's gin and tonic without a murmur from anyone. Tony H sat alone in the corner of the bar in his striped rugby shirt and characteristic headwear. One of the locals asked who that sad fellow in the corner was. 'Oh that's **Tommy** Hancock' his bar mate said in a loud voice. We all thought Tony was acting up for us all. It was much later that we discovered that his severe melancholic traits would eventually get the better of him. He took his life in Australia. I have never understood why many who give so much pleasure to us, do not seem to get very much themselves. The list is endless.

When we had all gone home the sound of a skylark filled the air with its glorious recital on high as the radio played that eternal desert island disc 'The Lark Ascending'. This prompted me to seek it at the local record shop. As I searched around the shelves the shop assistant asked me what I was looking for. 'A piece by Vaughan Williams' I replied. 'What's he singing?' was his response.

There were many social events to enjoy and it was the local Round Table that almost took over our lives at the time. I recently attended the 70th Anniversary of the founding of the one I joined early in my professional career. I was amazed that there were so many who recognised me at the dinner, it having been a good forty years since I had seen most of them. But it was John who had taken over the local garage after the great Mike Hawthorn had died who brought back the strongest memory. We had been at a black tie dinner when John crushed a glass in his hand he was about to raise for the loyal toast. He cut his hand quite badly severing a blood vessel or two in his thumb and forefinger. His blood spread across the table cloth where we were sitting. John had myself a veterinarian on one side and Tony a medical on the other. Tony was a leading medical practitioner in town. He said 'That looks rather nasty it will need some stitches. Unfortunately I don't have any suture materials with me'. I said that I had got mine in the car. So between us we sewed him up there and then. It was all well as John had had sufficient amounts of 'premedication' in the bar beforehand. So he sat through the procedure stoically. It was at the dinner forty years later that he showed me the scars of which he was rather proud!

I had been in the practice for seven years. Initially I had ideas about becoming a partner. The boss was a very kind man, his partner rather less so. His attitude to me was less sympathetic than I would have wished. He was a very good surgeon but did nothing to improve my skills. Above all they were all of a very strong religious way of life. I would like to think of myself as a Christian of the Church of England, albeit rather a private one. My appearances at church were largely restricted to occasions such as concerts, weddings, funerals and christenings. The boss did not try to push his views on me. He lead by example which is much more effective. He would always help others less fortunate than himself. My greatest mistake was to converse with his ex-naval partner in what I had become used to when in maritime company. Having spent my military career in close contact with the crews of the naval vessels in the dockyard near our RAF base the conversation in their mess was liberally spattered with what we now call 'strong language'. Swearing in other words. This was even more so when they came to our mess. I had assumed that all ex-naval personnel coloured their conversation this way. As a result I was written off by fifty percent of the partnership as that half had high religious standards. Forgiveness wasn't one of them. Some of the other veterinarians in the district had some strange traits. Two of whom met their end in tragedies. Betty ended up face down in the river after a weekend of over-indulgence. Harry a colleague in the Motor Club flew his aeroplane into the ground on the coast of France with fatal results. I was more fortunate in that I survived driving my car through a brick wall, of which more will be revealed later.

It was clear that the time had come to move on. The problem was that I did not want to leave all the friends I had in the area. The way round this was to become freelance and work as a locum until the next career opportunity came along. I kept my rooms in the local pub and set off on short spells standing in for veterinarians who were off on their holidays or who were incapacitated in some way. In the event I Iearned more in the three years working in this fashion than much of the rest of my work. It required a good deal of improvisation and a test of my map-reading capabilities. This time without my trusty motor rally navigator. I had to use whatever equipment and medicines that the practice used and had to get used to clients saying 'Oh you're not Mr . . . . '. Whoever their usual vet was; as if I didn't know.

Many of the motor vehicles I had to use were in a sorry state. One such was an Inspector Maigret-type Citröen in the final stages of its life. As I drove up the crowded High Street one morning, the steering wheel came adrift in my hands. This did attract a good deal of comment from those who saw me stranded in the middle of the road.

My own car was now an open top red sports car which I bought to enjoy driving and to improve my standing with the female population wherever I went.

On arrival at one practice in Surrey I was sent to the local Cricket Club to meet one of the practice partners. Peter was due to go into hospital for major surgery. The other partner was away to the drying out centre for rehabilitation. Peter was at the bar with his girl friend when his wife walked in. She announced to the assembled company that she was coming back to live with him. This was not greeted with joy by the current incumbent lady friend who walked out of the bar saying that she would raid the drugs cupboard in the practice and consume the contents. The remaining assistant in the practice Michael and I ran the four man practice for several weeks. I was back in mixed practice again. The principal's house was a few miles out in the country. It was a riding establishment which I visited regularly. One day I was asked to take a dead sheep into the practice surgery to carry out a post mortem examination. It was a sizeable beast that wouldn't go in the car boot which was full of all the kit necessary for a mixed practice. My make of car was said to have enough room in the back for two people as long as they were not over seven years old. The motor press also claimed that procreative activity was not possible in this vehicle. We proved that this was erroneous many times. So the dead sheep had to be sat in the passenger seat beside me. Unfortunately I was having trouble closing the folding roof of my car. So, I drove up the steep High Street on a busy Saturday morning in the sun. The double takes of the local population were a joy to see. Their first impression was that I had an old lady in a sheepskin coat alongside me on a hot morning. Anyone wanting to create such a sensation has only to find a dead sheep and drive it in an open sports car to achieve the same effect.

Another tour of duty took me back to my home county Kent working for Arthur a practice principal renowned for his somewhat bullying manner. He applied his rather aggressive approach to anyone who would submit to it. I knew he needed me in the practice, so when I refused to be intimidated by his character, he became quite friendly. He handed over a dog to me to do a caesarean operation with the command 'It's my neighbour's dog and it mustn't die'. It was a fourteen year old Labrador, and it didn't die. Arthur was famous in the practice for an episode which involved a young girl with a lame pony. He arranged to meet the girl on Bluebell Hill. He drove up the hill and saw a young lady with a pony standing by the roadside. He stopped and approached the rather timid girl with his customary gruff attitude. He examined the animal which was more a full sized horse than a small pony. 'Lame?' he said 'I can't find much wrong, take him up that path and back here'. After giving the girl a ticking off for moving on the inside as she turned, which would have obscured any faults evident on moving round he added 'I still can't see anything by way of lameness. I'll give it an injection and come back on Thursday'. At which he drove off up the hill only to find the girl he should have met at the top with her lame pony. The previous girl had just been standing around and was intimidated by this fearsome man. I hope he didn't send her a bill.

A short spell back at the old location allowed a little rest and a reunion with many old friends. One of whom was Jack a policeman. He drove a police car around all the major roads. He related his experiences in the local pub where we all played 'Tommy Dodd'. This was a game in which we all had three copper coins and elected to have between zero and three hidden in our hands. You had to guess the total concealed of all around the table. The person who guessed the total correctly dropped out and the next round began. This progressed until there was only one person left. He had to buy the next round of drinks.

Jack told us that he had pulled over a car that was being driven very erratically along the A3 sufficient to suspect the driver had been drinking to excess. He got the male suspect out onto the lay-by and subjected him to a breath test. The alcohol concentration of his exhalations was well above the limit. In fact it was off the scale. Jack then assumed that he had sufficient evidence to take the man in on a charge of driving under the influence. It was only then that the drunken person pointed out that he had not been driving. It was a left hand drive vehicle. Jack was too embarrassed to take the matter any further.

A national emergency changed everything in 1967. Foot and Mouth Disease (FMD) took hold of a large part of Shropshire and Cheshire. The then Ministry of Agriculture (MAFF) called for members of the veterinary profession to volunteer as Temporary Veterinary Inspectors (TVIs) to attempt to stem the progress of the disease through the country's livestock. The work rate was absolutely relentless as we went round farms examining animals for signs of the disease. Where clinical signs had been reported nearly every case was confirmed. All movement was prohibited and infected herds destroyed. Adjacent farms were inspected. At every farm we had to wear a full covering of protective clothing and were thoroughly disinfected on arrival and departure. Farmers took some pleasure in soaking us with very hot disinfectant solutions. There was little else to relieve their extreme anxiety. So much so that there were several suicides among the owners of the local stock. Compared with later outbreaks the number of animals involved was fewer as we were mainly dealing with dairy cattle, with some sheep and a few pigs. The awful thing about this was that most of the herds had been in farming families for generations and the farmers were completely wrecked by their losses. Worse still was the dreadful waiting for a diagnosis. In fact some were even relieved when they heard the worst.

During this experience I have to say that I changed my attitude to farmers. The ones I encountered were very brave, stoical in fact. They were helpful, cooperative and humane. The slaughtermen were also of sound quality. In their case if they had not been they would not have got the work. We buried most of the carcases, except where there was a problem with the water table. In these circumstances we had to build a massive fire.

One farm was in a very difficult situation in that it could only be accessed by way of another dairy farm which was an infected premises. The farmer in the isolated property was very stoical about it. He said that as long as he had his telephone he could talk to all his friends and neighbours and remain self-sufficient. Unfortunately, the very next day the digger we were using to bury the cows on the adjacent farm went straight through the telephone wires cutting him off completely. Repairs could not be carried out for quite a while. I was saved from the firing line as I was called away to another farm to follow up another case. This pace was absolutely frantic for many weeks, so much so that as I was driving back to our accommodation one night I heard the football results on the car radio. It was only then that I realised it was Saturday. I was subsequently moved to Nottinghamshire, after which the disease was eventually eliminated from the United Kingdom. When it came back in the early twenty first century I was in the RCVS building in London when I bumped into the RCVS President. He demanded to know why I was not out there fighting the latest Foot and Mouth outbreak. I explained that I was on the retired list of the Royal College and could no longer do clinical work. He said he would change all that and I could go. I would rather not I said as I had been an Inspector in the 1967/1968 outbreak. He understood.

After the Shropshire and Nottinghamshire episode I paid my first visit to a major International Veterinary Congress outside the UK. It was held by the World Veterinary Association (WVA) in Paris. It was also the first WVA Congress to include the World Small Animal Veterinary Association (WSAVA). An organisation I first attended in London in 1961 and was to become progressively more involved with over the years.

In Paris we combined social activities with our further education in the delightful surroundings and in great company. I have been going to most of the important veterinary gatherings around the world ever since.

As we sat in a splendid open air restaurant in the Champs Elysée we talked airily about our careers. This time the subject was not so much what we had done but what we planned to do next. As we saw off a number of delicious croissants and a good deal of first class cups of coffee, the subject turned to work for commercial companies. Working in industry had in the past been seen as a last resort with a danger of selling one's professional soul to the paymaster. But it became clear that things were changing as a number of highly respected members of our profession took very responsible jobs in research and as advisers to large business organisations. One colleague even suggested that I would be very suitable for such work. I thought of little else for days after this and decided to find a position to suit any talents I could convince the right sort of employer that I had. I did just that and my career changed radically yet again. I was offered the job of Veterinary Adviser to a major manufacturer of prepared foods for companion animals. I had landed on Mars!

Chapter 5

Other Jobs, Other Interests

Having been qualified some ten years, the next phase of my career was to be in the food industry. I became veterinary adviser to the Mars Group based in the Midlands where prepared foods were made for companion animals, horses, fish and cage birds. I had landed on Mars, an employer with very high standards and very caring for their 'associates' and all their animals. This involved looking after all the animals on site and engaging in investigations into nutrient requirements in health and disease. We made sure we did nothing unpleasant, only investigating clinical cases in the field. The Study Centre serviced all the Group's Companys around the world. There were growth trials and preference tests on own products and those of our competitors.

The animals we kept at our Centre were some of the happiest and healthiest I have encountered in my career. They were adequate proof that the feeding of foods prepared to the known nutrient requirements of each species was very effective.

My admiration for the Mars organisation remains at the very high level I recognised some forty years ago. It was a big plus that the many companies around the world were owned by a family. That is real people who took a close interest in what was going on around the world and those who worked for them; not some anonymous group you never saw or even knew who they were. Whilst they looked after us very well, they expected a great deal of effort in return. It was said that they paid us enough for two but expected us to work enough for three! Better that than the other way round any day.

Whilst most of my experiences in industry have to remain confidential, a few can be revealed without any problems. A canal ran beside one factory site. Here many ducks, geese and similar birds frolicked throughout the day. One duck was brought to me in a bad way. It had swallowed a fishing line and the hook had embedded deep down. We located it by radiography. Fortunately no-one had tried to pull it out, which would have caused serious damage. We anaesthetised the bird and cut the end off the hook and relieved the bird of the offending object. To everyone's delight it recovered almost immediately and was seen enjoying its life on the canal thereafter. Of all the veterinary work I did there, this was what I was mainly remembered for.

One case which went well beyond the limits of my expertise was a very friendly Newfoundland dog. It had jumped over the gate of its accommodation and left its hind leg behind. It had hung suspended for a very short time but this was enough to wreck its hock joint. Although it seemed remarkably stoical about its injury, something had to be done urgently. We took an x-ray picture to establish the extent of the damage. It was clear to me that this was a job for someone with a very high level of orthopaedic expertise if the joint was to be rebuilt. I telephoned Gary at my *Alma Mater*, The Royal Veterinary College in London. I explained the situation to him in detail. 'Oh, bring him in, I'll fix it. It'll be a fifteen minute job'. Newfie was put in my car and off we went some eighty miles down the A1 to the RVC. This was the only dog to go 'over the wall' from the Centre during my tour of duty. He was completely relaxed all the way there and back. In fact he seemed to enjoy the attention and the whole experience. I'm sure I would have been much more disturbed in such circumstances. Far from being 'a fifteen minute job', it took Gary about an hour and a quarter to complete the reassembly of the hock joint. However, the finished work was a piece of artistry. All the metal work caused Newfie no inconvenience at all. In fact he had to be held back from galloping all over the place on his return.

Once the hair had grown again you couldn't tell which leg it was that had been operated on.

In the middle of one night in October 1987 I had a telephone call. The so-called 'Hurricane' had seriously damaged the animal accommodation. My offer to come and attend to the matter was met with the information that all the local roads to the Centre were blocked by fallen trees. Although most of the dogs and cats had got out into the night, within a short time they had all got back in again and were now safe. I did get there the next day and all they really wanted was their food.

When one of the Mars brothers came to visit us at the Centre, I was put in charge of looking after Mrs M while the Directors had their meetings. After I had shown her round the units we went off to lunch in the village. On my return my superiors asked how I had got on. I reported favourably about the tour of our facilities, especially how much she enjoyed seeing the animals. When it came to the question of where I had taken her for lunch, they were horrified that we had gone for a pub lunch in the village. They were shocked we did not go to a classy restaurant in the next town. In fact Mrs M enjoyed her visit to the local pub so much she sent me a hand written letter of thanks. I kept this in my pocket ever afterwards.

I will forever be grateful to my employers for allowing me to devote time to veterinary organisations. It was at a Meeting at London Zoo in 1975 that I was approached by the President of the British Small Animal Veterinary Association (BSAVA). He mentioned that the Officers of the BSAVA had considered asking me to become their Treasurer. As I am not a financial person I declined explaining that the world is divided into Treasurer type people and Secretary types. I had been Honorary Secretary of one of the Association's Regions. 'Right' he said 'We'll put you down for Secretary'. So it was that I joined the BSAVA Officer team which was another turning point in my career.

As I completed my term of office as BSAVA Secretary I was asked to stand for Junior Vice-President (JVP). The BSAVA has what I believe to be an excellent system of moving the Officers along each year. Each position is held for one year at a time. The JVP moves to President Elect and then to President; all subject to election at the AGM. After one year in office the President moves to Senior Vice-President and leaves the team of Officers after another year. So, unless you are voted out (and it has happened) each Officer stays on board for four years. In effect you learn the job for two years and afterwards you school those who follow on. This works very well and is more effective than the arrangement in some countries where the President remains as President more or less indefinitely.

The only snag with my passage through the BSAVA system was that I became acutely ill a few months before taking over the top job. This was a serious worry for the President of the time who was concerned that he might have to do another year in office. The JVP was also worried that he might have to move up to President a year ahead of his scheduled time. In the event I left my gall bladder in the Infirmary and was restored to a state of health I had not enjoyed for a number of years. Although the staff from the cleaner to the Consultant Surgeon were excellent and looked after me very well, I was bored not being able to see animals of any kind except for a few birds out of the window when I was fit enough to walk around. I was interested to read in a medical journal of the beneficial effects of putting copies of fine art on the ward walls. It occurred to me that my interest in Companion Animals in Fine Art, a subject I have lectured on around the world for over thirty years, could be even more effective. It always seems to please people when they see these works and it wouldn't cost much to exhibit prints in hospitals. Clearly care must be taken not to expose any patients who were phobic about these creatures.

Whilst attending a World Small Animal Veterinary Association (WSAVA) Congress in Amsterdam I was walking past a room where the General Assembly was taking place. The President came out and saw me. He said that 'There was no one to represent the United Kingdom so would I be kind enough to stand in?' I did and at the next Congress in Barcelona I was asked to be Treasurer. ' No thank you' I said, so I became Secretary!

It was in Las Vegas in 1981 that I nearly caused a catastrophe. At the General Assembly I had assumed that I would take over the office of Honorary Secretary at the end of the formal part of the Meeting. The retiring Secretary thought otherwise. He was of the opinion that I became his successor at the beginning of the Meeting. Fortunately I had taken notes throughout the proceedings, so it was not too difficult to put together the minutes recording what had taken place. I learnt from this that different nations had different traditions.

Work with the WSAVA was quite demanding when there was a full time job to be given the attention required. Even so there were many pluses. In particular we met a large number of veterinary colleagues around the world, many of whom remain good friends. Although travel world-wide can be tiring, it is often enlightening and there are always surprises. One such happened in Las Vegas. We went to a concert which was held as a benefit for the jazz guitarist Wes Montgomery's brother who had advanced cancer. It was held in an enormous hotel and featured several world class performers. It was pure chance that we heard about this event. On arrival we asked one of the locals why this had not been advertised anywhere. 'The place is full isn't it?' was his reply. On to the stage walked Sarah Vaughan who was followed by others of her standard. Thinking that it could not get better we were stunned by the last man in. On to the stage strolled a man unannounced in a dark suit and a trilby hat. It was none other than Francis Albert Sinatra. He went into a song beginning with a line about New York being his 'kind of town'. Just as we were starting to sing along to this he changed it to 'New York, New York is a wonderful town' from the musical 'On the Town'. I had always enjoyed Sinatra's performances but to see him live was absolutely extraordinary when he was at the peak of his powers in the 1980s. His stage presence was very powerful indeed, without seeming to do very much. His charisma was undeniable. So much so that a Dutch colleague who was with us said that he had disliked his singing until he saw him in the flesh. If only that charm could be bottled up and sold, it would be snapped up by every lecturer around!

Many years later I dropped in to a matinee at the Savoy Theatre in London. When time allowed I would often go to matinees after engagements in the city. I would go up to the Box Office five minutes before the show was scheduled to begin and ask if I get anything off the ticket price for being old. This has often resulted in a big smile and some very good deals. After all the ticket would soon be worthless. This show was 'The Rat Pack' which had had quite good reviews, although no-one could be Dean Martin, Sammy Davis or the great Sinatra. I came back early from the bar at the interval and had a short chat with the lady sitting next to me. She asked me if I was enjoying the performance. I said that I was and it was all better than I had expected. Then I said the person playing Frank was good with all the right body language and quite a good voice. I explained that my knowledge was based on our Las Vegas experience in the 1980s. She turned out to be the mother of the person playing the part. For once I had said the right thing.

A small group of us were in Amsterdam for a Congress in the 1980s. We went out for a meal in the evening to an excellent restaurant in the centre of the city. We were in the middle of one of the best steaks I had enjoyed for a long time when we suddenly realised the significance of the name of the venue. It was an Argentine Steak Restaurant and we were at the height of the Falklands War. We called the waitress over to say how sorry we were. I said to the lady 'We must apologise to you as we are all English and we are currently at war with you'. She replied 'Wer dow yer think ouy cum frum' in a heavy Birmingham accent.

There were many strange episodes but one stands out in my memory. This time it was a Congress in Salzburg in Austria. A small group of us met at Munich Airport but the hand luggage was still in Scotland. The driver who was supposed to take us to Salzburg did not appear for another two and a half hours. One of my colleagues laid into the airport staff until he discovered there had been a major accident on the autobahn between the two cities. If the driver had arrived earlier we could have been involved in the pile up. On the way to Salzburg we took the mountain route along very high narrow winding roads. It became evident that the driver was very tired and was in danger of dropping off. We stopped him and got one of our female colleagues to sit beside him at the front of the vehicle. This was a mistake as she was rather attractive and diverted his attention from the forward direction of our journey. Even so we managed to get to Salzburg unharmed and the driver took us to our hotel. As time was short the driver offered to take us to the location of the evening dinner, the Hotel Schlussel. We get to the hotel only to discover they had never heard of the dinner we were due to attend. I showed the manager the invitation with all the details. He informed us that it was the Restaurant Schlussel we required. 'Where is that' we asked. 'It is two kilometres downstairs' he said. You must have a very deep cellar I thought. In fact it was down the mountainside and it was pitch dark. Our driver had gone home so we had to walk down the narrow winding road with no lighting at all. About half way down a vehicle drove past us at considerable speed. My friends climbed up the bank on their side and I disappeared over the edge on mine. I did not know if I was going to fall five feet or two thousand feet. They thought I had gone for ever. I emerged unharmed and we made our way to the dinner at the restaurant which eventually appeared. I was summoned to the top table and my friends sat below. They kept trying to indicate something to me. This turned out to be that not only was I the speaker but they do before dinner speeches rather than those after the meal. So I told them how we got there, which they found entertaining.

The Presidency of the World Small Animal Veterinary Association, the international version of the BSAVA, is normally for two years. You take over at one World Congress and hand over two years later. The national member association hosts the Congress in the location of each year. As the WSAVA Congress is now an annual event, there are three in each Presidential term of office. I became President in San Francisco and passed the Chain of Office on in Rome. The Congress in between was in Vienna.

The Congress in San Francisco held in 1990 was hosted by The American Animal Hospital Association (AAHA). It was where I was due to take over as President. This was the year of one of that city's devastating earthquakes, when one of the motorway bridges collapsed. It was important to make sure the venue was still there and there were no related problems which could prejudice our meeting. It was crucial that I went out there to check everything. Time was short so I was flown out there for the day. It took a day to get there and a day to get back which was the longest day trip of my life. Fortunately the newly built hotel where all this was going to take place was in a stable area and had been constructed to take the movements brought about by the San Andreas fault.

Legendary astronaut Neil Armstrong gave the opening address. In common with many really high-powered individuals, he turned out to be a pleasant self-effacing person with a sense of humour. He obviously had a genuine affection for the veterinary profession.

It was at this meeting that I met a long standing veterinary friend who I had met at several meetings in the USA. She even named her practice cat after me. One day I telephoned her veterinary hospital from the UK. The receptionist asked who was calling. I simply said it was Andrew Edney. 'Yikes' she screamed 'the cat's escaped and he's calling from England'. Well it was a good story for my Presidential address.

I went to a total of eighteen countries in the two and a half years I was President of the WSAVA. It was when we were coming back from America that a drama occurred at Atlanta airport. It was at the outbreak of the Gulf war in 1991. We were at a social evening at the North American Veterinary Conference in Orlando, Florida. All military personnel were ordered to return to their station without delay. It is extraordinary how all sorts of rumours were going round as a result of this. We were told that Orlando Airport was closed, which it wasn't; that all flights to Europe were cancelled, which they weren't and that all flights into the UK were being turned away, which they weren't. However the airport was almost empty when we got there the next morning and we did get a flight to Atlanta to begin our journey home. We sat on the perimeter track there for quite a while and by then it was dark. There were few passengers in our part of the plane. One who was nearby turned and said 'I may be hearing things but there seems to be someone banging on the floor below as if they are stuck in the luggage hold'. I said you aren't imagining it I can hear a person shouting 'Help, help, someone get me out of here'. I intercepted the Chief Steward who was rushing about his business. He did not want to know and said he must complete his procedure as the Captain was waiting to take off. Somewhat uncharacteristically, I shouted that I must insist as someone's life could be in danger. This time the steward came over to where we were sitting so he could hear the banging and shouting. His face suddenly went a strange colour and he disappeared onto the flight deck. The doors of the hold then opened up but they obscured my view. The passenger near the window had a slightly better view. I asked him what he could see. He said there were two people in uniform who were supporting a third away to the airport buildings. When the steward came back into the cabin he did not want to discuss the matter. I said that I just wanted to ask a couple of quick questions. 'Was there a person locked in the hold below?'. 'Yes' was his reply. 'He would have died of anoxia if he had stayed there?'. 'No, he would have frozen to death as the temperature is around minus 50 degrees'. 'Then we saved his life?'. 'Yes' was his brief but stunning answer.

My work with the Open University finally focused on what is known as The Humanities. That is what I would call The Arts. This eventually led to a Masters Degree in History. This took three years, the first of which included my efforts to complete my Doctorate in Veterinary Medicine, which had taken rather longer than I had anticipated. My DVetMed thesis was finally accepted and my MA dissertation an examination of propaganda in the cinema during the second world war also got the blessing of the examiners. My earlier OU work studied many aspects of fine art but it was representational art which appealed to me most. This came in very useful when I was given the job of editing a magazine called *Pedigree Digest*. This was a publication for all those whose interest was in all aspects of companion animals. The previous editor had used many examples of fine art which featured such creatures on the cover. It was only when I researched this subject in depth I realised how vast it is. It became a favourite topic for lectures. These started in Amsterdam and have remained in my repetoire ever since. The piece I wrote on this subject is included in Chapter 6.

When the time came to retire from my work with the Mars Group in 1986, I remained as a consultant with them. This was supposed to be for two years but finished up as eight. This proved to be timely as I had become involved in a number of other organisations. I worked for the World Health Organisation in Geneva, Cyprus and San Marino. I was known as an early Dr Who at the time. I edited two reports of our work largely because I was the only member of the group whose native language was English.

Another group of us formed what was to be known as The Group for the Study of the Human Animal Bond. This rather clumsy title was changed to The Society for Companion Animal Studies (SCAS). This has now become an important organisation contributing to The International Association of Human-Animal Interaction Organisations (IAHAIO) with regular conferences around the world.

SCAS has a Pet Bereavement Support Service which helps those who have lost their companion animals. This is now administered by The Blue Cross animal welfare charity. I have been involved as a Governor/Trustee of this major charity for nearly twenty years. In my view it is one of the most important such charities which has been effective since over a hundred years ago. I became The Blue Cross Chairman in the late 1990s. The day after I took on this role we were due to open our new Animal Hospital in Merton in South London. Queen Elizabeth the Queen Mother did the opening ceremony. She was pleased to do this as she had been a patron of what was then known as Our Dumb Friends League in 1926 before we changed our title to The Blue Cross. She did a wonderful job and was charming to all and showed great interest in all our animals and she was ninety eight at the time! When she came to leave a young lad called Nathan was to give her a bouquet of flowers on her departure. He was asked to bow down when he did this, but we had not told him to stop bowing down when he had done it. His photograph with his head nearly on the ground was a full page in one of the tabloid newspapers the next day!

Queen Elizabeth The Queen Mother opened the new Blue Cross Animal Hospital in Merton South London in 1999. Her Majesty was presented with a bouquet of flowers by a very loyal young Nathan Goodwin. Picture by Mirrorpix

On a lecture tour around Europe I am speaking in Bruno, Slovakia

With Astronaut Neil Armstrong left, who opened the World Congress
in San Francisco when I took over the Presidency in 1990

In Australia tending a kangaroo in McClellan Park, Adelaide

Making my Presidential after dinner speech at the British Small
Animal Veterinary Association Congress in London

James Alfred Wight left, who wrote under the name of James Herriot receiving the WSAVA Award from me at the Golden Fleece in Thirsk in 1992

Myself receiving the WSAVA International Award for Service to the Profession at the Congress in Jerusalem in 1996

I hand over the Presidential Badge of Office to Professor Akira
Takeuchi from Japan at the World Congress in Rome in 1992 (Cropped)

I resist the temptation to stop the car and amend this sign in Essex.
Loves green certainly, but common?

Chapter 6

Companion Animals in Fine Art

The More You Look, The More You See

Following on from my experiences editing *Pedigree Digest* which always featured a work of art with a companion animal on the cover I worked on this subject for many years. Doing an Arts Degree with the Open University and my years as an Officer of the World Small Animal Veterinary Association (WSAVA) helped a great deal. As I had visited a total of eighteen countries as President I had the opportunity to go to most of the major Art Galleries in the world.

I have been giving presentations on the subject of 'Companion Animals in Fine Art' for more than thirty years now. I am encouraged by the fact that they have gone down well all round the world, especially amongst the veterinary and human medical world. The only worries expressed have been a number of people telling me that whenever they go to any exhibition displaying these works they immediately start to look for the dog, cat, rabbit or horse. The great benefit of this is that the number of works which include these animals is limitless. As a result I get advised about new examples all the time.

Representational art is a reflection of the way we have lived over the years. As a result, our relationship with companion animals is well recorded. What is startling about this is the skill of some of the observers who recorded the characteristics of dogs and cats with astonishing accuracy long before photography became available. In addition to this the key role of the dog in our society and to a lesser extent the cat, comes through as central to the lives of many different types of people. What we usually consider a very modern phenomenon, is clearly of much longer standing than was previously thought. The immense power of what we have come to call the human/companion animal bond is vividly illustrated in an enormous variety of works. This relationship is what keeps those of us in companion animal veterinary practice in business.

Paintings interest most people to some extent. This is not just because of the thought that millions of dollars or so can be spent on a flower painting by Vincent Van Gogh; newsworthy though that may be. Value is always more important than cost. Many of us have one or two original works of some sort in our homes. The image the mind retains is usually more powerful than a print or even a photograph. It is easy for me to see how anyone with a strong interest in dogs and cats can become preoccupied with the subject of pets in paintings.

There is now medical evidence to show that displaying fine art in hospitals helps patients to recover. As most people seem to find art works with companion animals in them to be pleasing, it would be fascinating to do some research to see if their effect on the walls of hospital wards would be strongly beneficial.

Paintings of Individual Animals

It is not just paintings of the animals themselves which demand attention, although there are some wonderful examples (Secord 1992). 'The Shepherd's Dog' by Rosa Bonheur, 'Pomeranian Bitch and Puppy' and 'Setter' by Thomas Gainsborough and 'King Charles Spaniel' by Gysbert van der Kuyl, are paintings of dogs on their own. The latter, painted in the mid-17th century, could be a relative of Manet's King Charles Spaniel in the National Gallery of

Art in Washington DC. Both would easily pass as representatives of the breed today. There are many works on the same lines by Sir Edwin Landseer, Maud Earl, Arthur Wardle and the Stretton and Emms families. The Dog Museum of America has many splendid examples. There are no better examples of'catness' in paintings and drawings than in the works of Théophile-Alexandre Steinlen in the early 20th century and Lesley Fotherby today.

Dogs and Cats in Paintings

What is perhaps more exciting, is to try to establish why artists put companion animals in their serious works. Dogs may appear as part of the composition; both dogs and cats can be included as part of the social scene (from refugees and tramps to aristocrats and royalty); as symbols, especially of qualities such as fidelity; as illustrations of the work they do such as shepherding, herding and hunting; as carefully observed behavioural studies and expressions of what we have come to call the human/companion animal bond. In all these instances the artists could simply have liked dogs and cats or included those they owned as their subject.

Really Looking at Paintings

It may seem rather strange to claim that there are benefits for veterinary surgeons in the careful examination of works of art. If nothing else it helps to train us in simple observation. It is surprising how many things come to light even in works we think we are familiar with. The pleasure we get from looking at a photograph of say, Willy Lott's Cottage which appears in 'The Hay Wain' or the Bridge at Asnières (both real locations) would soon flag. But the wonderful representations of these by John Constable and Georges Seurat can last a lifetime.

An important strategy when visiting an exhibition of fine art or attending a collection in a museum is to select carefully what looks promising and study it in detail. If possible it is a good plan to return on another day and look again. It is astonishing how much more you can see that way. Trying to examine every work on display in the Hermitage in St Petersburg or the Metropolitan in New York City would quickly lead to viewing fatigue. The more familiar we think we are with a work the less likely we are to look at it closely. It is extraordinary how many visitors to galleries spend more time looking at the label than the work itself.

If the viewer imagines they are a veterinarian examining an animal for a health check or a judge at Crufts Dog Show responsible for picking the next 'Best in Show', they will get some idea the degree of concentration required to get the most out of fine art. Look at it from every angle, from close up to from across the room, even the next room in some cases! Look at the colours, look at the composition (where is the eye led?). Look at the balance or lack of it, assess the draughtsmanship and then look at the subject.

A recent exhibition I went to had over two hundred works on display. My membership of an Arts organisation allowed me free entry on several occasions. It is extraordinary how much more you see on the return visits.

Composition

Dogs are very often included in paintings as a key part of the composition. They have two things about them which help artists. Firstly they are normally at ground level. Because of this they bring some activity to the lower reaches of the work. Full length portraits often benefit from having a little canine action at floor level. In what is known as 'The Arnolfini Marriage', Jan van Eyck placed a bright eyed little terrier at the feet of the newly married or possibly betrothed couple. Our eyes are lead down to dog level by the folds in the lady's dress to the feet of the man on her right side. The dog is there primarily for symbolic reasons, being a symbol of fidelity but he enriches this glorious work by his animated appearance in the foreground.

The second canine characteristic which artists make free use of is that dogs are mostly pointed at the front! Those with a tail have this to help in that direction also. Because of this they can lead the eye into areas the artist wants us to concentrate upon. They help to provide a great deal of movement in otherwise static pictures. A late work by Thomas Gainsborough usually known as 'The Morning Walk', to be found in The National Gallery in London, is a wedding portrait of a Mr and Mrs Hallett, a fashionable couple in the 1780s. The eye is caught by a magnificent large white dog to our left. The Samoyed-like animal gazes up at the couple and draws our view to a point where the bride's left hand shows us her new ring. The work is enriched by the handsome dog and it is easy to see how reduced the effect would be without him by masking vision with the palm of the hand. Even if the dog was on the other side of the painting it would lose something as the eye is normally led into the work from the bottom left. Only a few minutes walk from this work in the National Gallery in London is 'The Hay Wain' by John Constable. This time the dog in the foreground directs our eye with his tail to a cottage and with his muzzle, takes us towards some people in a cart which stands in the river. The artist realised that a human figure with a barrel which he had included beside the cart was superfluous and painted it is out, although it is just becoming visible again as the paint wears away over the years.

The fact that dogs vary in size and shape more than any other mammalian species gives artists endless opportunities. The tiny puppy in Manet's 'Gare St Lazare' is essential to the work. Equally, at the other end of the scale, a very large Mastiff gives Anthony van Dyck the chance to make the son who was to become King Charles II look very impressive indeed in 'The Eldest Children of Charles I'.

The Social Scene

One of the striking aspects of dog and cat ownership is that it is a characteristic of all social strata in the Western world and beyond. Early Dutch genre paintings show everyday life in the humblest dwellings. They almost invariably have a dog or cat featured somewhere, sometimes several. The same applies to all other levels, including Royalty, kings, queens and princes, dukes and their families, merchants, labourers, those in gambling houses and naughtier venues and schoolchildren. Scenes in churches frequently have dogs nosing around the naves, some even relieving themselves against the masonry.

Many medieval illuminated manuscripts, some dating from the 13th century and before are very lively showing animals of all kinds mostly well cared for. A 15th century triptych by Rogier van der Weyden shows a little white dog in a deeply religious work. What is extraordinary about this work is that it is obviously well groomed, looking very much like an early ancestor of a recent Crufts Dog Show winner. In the same museum in Munich there is another work to astonish us. It shows the 'Virgin Ascending the Steps of the Temple' with the usual array of saints and donors. What is really amazing is that two small dogs play between the two groups. They play-fight very conspicuously in the centre of the painting. The dominant dog dominates, not only the other dog but the whole foreground of the Temple. He is neatly groomed and has a tail fashioned as a pom-pom; and this work dates from 1465.

Two examples illustrate the limits of the social spectrum. Honoré Daumier painted 'Les Fugitifs' about 100 years ago. It is a timeless representation of all refugees. They are anonymous as they come over a small hill to our right. The column forms a shallow 'V' shape as it turns to disappear through the hills to our left. At the point of the 'V' walks a dog slightly to one side but clearly part of the group. It does not look deprived or badly treated, but Daumier's masterstroke is to show its head bowed down as if taking on the unseen burdens of the humans suffering persecution. A tiny alteration of the angle of the dog's head and the work could have become just ordinary.

In the National Portrait Gallery in London you can see King Edward VII's Queen when she was Princess Alexandria of Denmark. In this painting by Sir Luke Fildes she has in her lap a very aristocratic looking Japanese Chin dog. The 'constantly startled' look of the breed is captured, but Alexandria remains serene.

Play

Those of us who spend our lives in the company of animals will know the behavioural traits they exhibit when playing. Cats play with wool, ping-pong balls, anything dangling in front of them and anything they can chase. Dogs have a very characteristic 'play bow' position as an invitation to frolic. This behaviour is shown in very many works of art including grave figures from ancient times. An excellent example can be seen in what is otherwise a conventional 'Music Party' by Jacob Ochterveldt in the National Gallery, London.

A lady stands at the keyboard with her back to the viewer. A musician is about to accompany her on the viola da gamba. It is a wonderfully tranquil scene, static even. However, the work comes to life by two dogs which occupy the foreground. The red and white individual on the left is in the classic 'play bow' position. On the other side, bringing a splendid tension across the whole picture, a little black and white dog responds with what can be described as a 'catch me if you can' stance.

Work

There are countless examples of working animals, be they hunting, herding, shepherding, ratting, retrieving game and guarding in paintings. A work which says a great deal about animals working with man is 'The Return of the Hunters' by Pieter Brueghel the elder which can be seen in Vienna along with many other works by this extraordinary artist. The motley collection of dogs look as despondent as the hunters who have not done very well. The whole group almost in silhouette produce an unforgettable effect. In my view it is worth going to Vienna just to see the room full of Brueghels in the Kunsthistoriches Museum. If you owned a single work by any of this family you wouldn't need any others, you would find something new in it every day. I brought this point up with a guide in the Museum of Fine Arts in Budapest as we stood in front one of these paintings. 'Yes' she said 'That's what the cleaner always says'.

Symbolism and the Human/Companion Animal Bond

It is easy to find plenty of examples of dogs used as symbols of fidelity in paintings 'The Arnolfini Marriage' (which may be a betrothal) by Jan van Eyck mentioned above, is full of symbolism. The bright eyed terrier is included as a symbol of lasting fidelity. Rather more obvious use of a dog in this way is evident in many Victorian works. In 'Sympathy' by Briton Rivière, a large Collie type dog rests its head on the knee of an unfortunate prisoner sitting in the corner of his cell. He holds his head in remorse and has his arm in a sling, suggesting that he has been imprisoned after a fight. Whatever he may have done, his dog remains faithful. Whilst this may strike the present day viewer as rather kitsch, there is no denying the painter knew about dogs. In 'The Order of Release 1746' by John Everett Millais, a survivor of the 1745 rebellion in Scotland has just been released by the English redcoat turnkey. He falls into the arms of his devoted wife and is greeted by his equally faithful dog. The dog jumps up in greeting to complete a triangular composition. Again the highlander's arm is in a sling, which is very conspicuous making another triangular form. What is not immediately obvious is that the dog is licking his master's hand which clasps that of his wife. All of this is absolutely right technically, symbolically and as a precise observation of canine behaviour. Similar scrutiny of another painting by Briton Rivière reveals a comparable detail. In 'His Only Friend' a vagrant child lies by a milestone. He is in a bad way, consumptive perhaps and probably terminal. His dog, his only friend, looks reasonably well. Possibly the dog was given food while the boy went hungry? He sits rather uncomfortably at his side and again licks the hand of his expiring master.

There are countless portraits of children with pet animals. Picasso's 'Child with Dove' crystallizes the concept admirably. Other works show clearly how awkward animals can be when embraced by children. Sir Joshua Reynolds portrayal of 'Princess Sophie Mathilde' shows a very young infant who has trapped a small dog with her arm. She lies on the ground with the dog's teeth dangerously close to her face. How the animal is restrained can be seen to effect how uncomfortable it feels. It only has its teeth to defend itself. Whereas cats have five things to hit you with.

Two contrasting works by Renoir show a cat which is absolutely relaxed and another that would certainly rather be somewhere else. The animal in 'Girl with Cat' in the National Gallery in Washington DC is not supported in a way it can feel at ease. Similar portraits by Peroneau and Gainsborough show how not to hold a cat. They need to be comfortably supported underneath. In contrast Renoir's 'Sleeping Girl with Cat' in the Clark Institute Williamstown, Massachusetts, is one of the wonders of our subject, showing perfect harmony between cat and human. The girl sits asleep in a chair with the cat on her lap. It dozes with its foreleg outstretched. The ultimate statement of the rapport between animal and human, the Human/ Companion Animal Bond, is where the girl's hand and the cat's paw are gently intertwined.

Further Reading

Clutton-Brock J (1988) 'The British Museum Book of Cats: Ancient and Modern' pub by Britsh Museum Press, London

Edney A T B (1991) 'Seeking Them Out: Dogs in Paintings' Kennel Gazette **112** 42-45 pub by The Kennel Club London

Edney A T B (1999) 'Cat: Wild Cats to Pampered Pets' pub by Evergreen an imprint of Taschen UK and by Watson Guptill in New York City

Foucart-Walter E and Rosenburg P (1987) 'The Painted Cat: The Cat in Western Painting from the Fifteenth to the Twentieth Century' pub by Rizzoli New York City

Fountain R and Gates A (1984) 'Stubbs Dogs: The Hounds and Domestic Dogs of the Eighteenth Century as seen through the Paintings of George Stubbs' pub by Ackermann London

Nash J (1992) 'Themes in Art: Cats' pub by Zwemmer London

Rubin JH (2003) 'Impressionist Cats and Dogs' pub by Yale University Press New Haven and London

Secord W (1992) 'Dog Painting 1840-1940: A Social History of the Dog in Art' pub by Antique Collectors Club UK

Secord W (2000) 'Dog Painting: The European Breeds' pub by Antique Collectors Club UK

Secord W (2001) 'A Breed Apart: The Art Collections of the American Kennel Club and The American Kennel Club Museum of the Dog' pub by Antique Collectors Club UK; American Kennel Club USA

Chapter 7

AND WHILE YOU'RE HERE

It was a dark and stormy night, and I was rushing to an emergency call. It was very late and I was trying to marshal my thoughts on what I might be about to encounter. It was then that I drove my car through a brick wall!

It could have happened to anyone. Even though I was on a road that I was reasonably familiar with I had mistakenly thought a T-junction was a crossroads (I was not the first, and will probably not be the last to do this). By the time I came to rest, it was.

I was as new to driving as I was to the veterinary profession and it was in the days before seat belts were a legal requirement. The property I was approaching was hidden by a dip in the road. When I looked up I saw the wall getting bigger very rapidly. I did manage to steer the part of the car I was in through the large wooden gate attached to the wall. The rest of the vehicle knocked the wall down. My chest hit the steering wheel and pushed the steering column through the windscreen just before my head did the same.

By some miracle I was fortunate to emerge from the now wedge shaped Morris 1000 with superficial but very bloody cuts to my face. We all know that a little blood looks like a lot of blood and a lot of blood looks like a heck of a lot of blood. However, what really hurt was the Winchester (a heavy two-litre glass bottle) of sulphamezathine solution which had hit me on the head as the contents of the boot were projected into the car. Vets of my vintage will know that 'sulphamez' contained a dye called Brilliant Green, it was the standard treatment for 'Foul in the Foot' in cattle.

I pulled my way from the wreckage and made my way to the house on the property I had invaded. It bore a striking resemblance to the Bates Motel on a bad night. I tapped tentatively on the door which opened to reveal a rather excitable lady from Northern Europe. She let out a fearsome shriek as she saw this person covered in blood and Brilliant Green, with fragments of windscreen glass forming what appeared to be a halo around his head. I uttered 'I've had a bit of an accident. Can I use your telephone please?'

At this point her husband shouted from upstairs to enquire what was going on. On being appraised of the situation he uttered the memorable words 'He hasn't damaged the wall has he?'

They allowed me to telephone the garage to recover the car and then my boss to deal with the emergency call-out. The garage man arrived and said immediately 'Course it's a write-off'. The principal of our practice seemed to be the only person concerned with my state of health. 'Are you all right?' he said 'Don't worry I'll do the call and my wife will get you home'.

After an extensive wash my face assumed a pale colour. It was at this point that it became clear to my new acquaintances that I was a vet. Then I heard my first and worst 'while you're here' request. 'Oh we have been thinking of getting a vet in to look at the dog' the lady of the house said. Well I don't dislike German Shepherd Dogs, but this one was hard work. My slightly colourful, bizarre appearance hadn't helped.

The dog had the full set of canine aggressions as well as anal furunculosis and a chronic ear problem. Worst of all the owners were somewhat afraid of him.

The lesson learned from all this was that when you hear the words 'Oh and while you're here will you . . . . etc?' it will be something tricky and will take twice as long as the time you had allowed for the visit. We had to go through this every few weeks from then on.

A year or so later on a pleasant summers day I was driving past the site of my accident. Someone had knocked down 'my' wall. It had only just happened and the driver was looking very pale sitting in his driving seat with his white knuckles still clutching the wheel. I stopped to see if I could help. 'The brakes failed didn't they mate.' he said. I was just about to express my sympathy and relate my experiences the winter before when the excitable lady appeared. She saw the wreckage and the collapsed wall, and me standing alongside. As she was about to launch into attack mode on me I drew attention to the fact that I was merely a passer by and that I did not normally drive a three-ton army truck. She then tore into the military gent who was responsible on this occasion. She shouted at him saying that he ought to be ashamed of himself as it was broad daylight, whereas with me it had been a 'night not fit for the dog'.

There is a roundabout there now.

Chapter 8

IN MY OPINION

Edney's Aphorisms

Some points I have learned from experience which may prevent others making the same mistakes. This will then leave them free to make their own.

1) The more you look the more you see, be it in clinical medicine, fine art or everyday life.
2) Never get between two parties fighting: they will both hit you.
3) Things are not what they were: they rarely were what we think they were.
4) Go to a court of law as a spectator before you have to go as a participant.
5) Make friends before you need them.
6) Nobody loves the editor.
7) Resist writing to the newspapers, unless you have something important to say. Important to the rest of the world that is, not just you.
8) You lose some and you lose some.
9) It is usually best to avoid things 'folklorico' when abroad.

10) To find out what is interesting anywhere, it is best to get local knowledge.

11) The EEC was a good idea until it became the EC: The EU is awful.

12) The EU is an acceptable concept but only if it is run entirely by the English, everyone speaks English, the single currency is Sterling, we all drive on the proper side of the road (ours), play cricket and take tea at 4 o/c in the afternoon.

13) Be as good as your word.

14) Play to the rules; do not argue with the umpire or referee.

15) It's winning that matters. With due respect for 14 above.

16) Football, rugby, tennis, golf are only games they don't really matter that much: but cricket is cricket.

17) The first rule of public relations is to get peoples' names right.

18) Guns are for blowing holes in things or threatening to, not much else.

19) Even pointing a toy gun at someone can look just as threatening.

20) Never try to be amusing at security checks.

21) Keep away from airports in July and August (Northern Hemisphere).

22) The shortest queue (line) is often the slowest moving.

23) Don't keep people hanging around unless you have to.

24) Try not to get upset about matters over which you have no control, like the weather or the opposite sex.

25) Never be more than a quarter of an hour late for an appointment.

26) Experts who are very experienced can say 'they don't know' occasionally and we will still believe they are very wise.

27) Believe in yourself. If you don't no-one else will.

28) Keep it short. No-one was ever criticised for too short a speech (Lord Birkett).

29) Never start with an apology.

30) Don't think you can't do it.

31) The most difficult person to convince can be yourself.

32) Above all always deliver.

33) Don't become a food faddist.

34) The world is divided into those who return books you lent them and those who mean to.

35) Humanity is divided into plainsmen and forest people.

36) The world is divided into the British and foreigners.

37) Never gamble with more than you can afford to lose.

38) There is no such thing as having too much money.

39) Improving your house always costs more than you thought it would and can take much longer.

40) People can deceive themselves with the concept of a Barbeque Summer. Don't they know a BBQ is a Rain Making Ceremony?

41) People often ask me 'do I like dogs or cats'. It is like asking if I like breathing out or breathing in

42) Beware of people who say they don't care how much your services will cost. They are probably not going to pay you.

43) Your ultimate ambition should be to get paid for doing what you enjoy doing, in your own time.

44) If you go to a riotous party always aim to be the last to get drunk, never the first.

45) Agree at an early stage who is going to drive you home after the party.

46) Treat the opposite sex as people, even if you think they are another species.

47) Military people stay military for ever.

48) Don't write off older people, they are experienced, more mature and often wealthier.

49) Youngsters normally grow into older people. Not the other way round.

50) Never say 'Cheer up, it may never happen' to anyone looking sad. It might already have happened.

51) Never tell a recently bereaved owner who has just lost their pet they must 'get another right away'. Only they know when the time is right.

52) The medicals are taught to 'Observe, observe and observe again' the same applies to veterinarians and the rest of us. See (1) above.

53) Writing is hard work but can be fulfilling, rewarding even.

54) Be a good listener, think about what someone is saying to you rather than just your witty reply.

55) Respect all of the animal kingdom, including people.

56) Most associations are run by fewer than 1% of their membership, i.e. by those who turn up.

57) The one who leads from the front can be the first to be shot.

58) If you buy a white car it will only look clean once.

59) In the winter all the trees look as if they are made of wood.

60) Answer all invitations even if you can't go. Reply in writing if they are written.

61) Once you have original paintings, even quite ordinary works, you won't just want prints or reproductions.

62) Self pity is a luxury few can afford.

63) Many people do little more than 'read the pictures 'in any publication.

64) It is easy to assume that just because you have told someone something they will know it. Often they have no recollection or get your advice wrong.

65) Equally, just handing out a leaflet does not always add much to their total knowledge.

66) Be as generous with praise as you are with your criticism.

67) Try to give something back if you have been at all successful in life.

68) Somewhere there is someone who designs pencil sharpeners that nip off the point just when you thought it was about right.

69) I have yet to meet a male who liked women to have their hair cut short.

70) There are not many happy endings in life, so make the most of any that come your way.

71) To be disillusioned you have to be illusioned in the first place.

72) He who says 'Anything for a quiet life' seldom gets one.

73) There is always someone worse at it than you are, be it ski-ing, golf, dancing or just struggling through life.

74) It's easy to laugh at other people's misfortunes, try laughing at your own.

75) Unfavourable weather can be a nuisance, depressing, dangerous even but it is not the Black Death coming in from the sea.

76) If it don't rain we don't eat, as they say in Australia.

77) One day I may meet a farmer who had a good season, but I doubt it.

78) It is equally unlikely that you will encounter anyone who thought the 1974 British boundary changes were a good thing.

79) We were all pleased that we got Rutland back and didn't have to pay all our rates to Leicestershire.

80) Everyone should have some 'nerves' before they get up to speak before an audience. If you haven't you aren't taking it seriously enough. Then you use that adrenalin level to power your presentation.

81) Your audience wants you to be good. You only have yourself to beat.

82) Morning people are best not living with night birds.

83) Engaged couples should spend a weekend sailing in a medium sized yacht as a test of their loyalty and compatability.

84) Only inflict your holiday snaps, films, videos on people you don't like.

85) Having a cold nose is not always a sign of good health; it's cold when you are dead.

86) People do not like jokes being made about the work they do.

87) Don't make fun of peoples names.

88) Equally do not saddle your children with silly names for which they will suffer later on.

89) Everyone needs feedback (let me know).

90) When you read an inaccurate report of something you have been present at, such as a football match or a play, you wonder about the reporting of world affairs.

91) All music, drama and art was modern once.

92) There is precious little classical music that is listenable which postdates Sibelius.

93) Art and music are for everyone not just the elite.

94) Because someone likes opera, chamber music, symphonies and the like does not prohibit them from enjoying pop music, rock and roll, heavy metal or jazz.

95) Some people put to Shakespeare early in life never recover.

96) Shakespeare works as theatre with the young. The poetry comes later.

97) Pet animals are an emotional investment of the highest order. You realise the strength of the Human/Companion Animal Bond when it is severed. When that happens it is a bereavement for the owner.

98) Don't bother to stand up on aircraft until they open the doors.

99) Trains and planes are rarely late when you are.

100) Passengers on a plane will watch a video of the safety drill but ignore a live person in front of them.

101) When you are in the garden, attic, toilet or bath the telephone you have left somewhere will stop ringing a microsecond before you reach it.

102) The sexes are different, thank goodness.

103) It is better to read newspapers from the back page forwards. They tend to be less depressing that way.

104) Write things down. If Mozart had done everything on the phone to his father we would not have known much about his life.

105) After months without an invitation, several will arrive for the same night.

106) If you can keep your head when all about you are losing theirs, you probably haven't been fully informed of the situation. Or you don't understand it.

107) If you put old newspapers on the floor for your dog's muddy paws or your shoes, or in a drawer lining, storys in them will become irresistible.

108) The great English summer sport is digging up the roads. Those doing the digging always seem to be on holiday. You see Road Works signs all along the Motorways but seldom is there anyone doing anything.

109) The only way to find out if there is life after death is to die. If there isn't you won't know, but it won't matter. Just in case there is it is best to behave yourself throughout life.

110) If just thinking about fleas, lice and other parasites makes you itch how many skin problems are psychosomatic? Are you feeling itchy now?

111) In any debate hold a few cards in reserve.

112) If you want to bring up a really contentious issue at a long meeting keep it as late in the agenda as you can.

113) One day you may get the weather on holiday that people usually say you should have been there for last week, but not often.

114) It is too easy to be rude on the telephone.

115) A great compliment to a child is to talk to it as an adult.

116) Conversely to insult an adult, talk down to it.

117) When the English talk about 'it' (isn't it wonderful, awful or whatever?) they mean the weather. Everyone else is referring to sex.

118) Eating can be a joy, fun even, but the science of nutrition can be deadly dull.

119) A club for flawed geniuses would have a long list of candidates for membership.

120) People can be very territorial about theatre seats, their place in line or on the beach.

121) Computers do what you tell them to do, not always what you want them to do.

122) Always let dogs or cats have a look at you first before you handle them.

123) Cats know when they are on a good thing.

124) There is no magic, it is all a trick.

125) English is the world language. This is very good for anyone publishing around the world.

126) It is extraordinary that the most widely used language in the world can often be mangled by its owners, the English

127) Don't believe everything you read in the newspapers.

128) It is not that everyone who keeps pets is crackers, it is just that many of those who are nutters have animals.

129) All holiday is no holiday.

130) Many people who retire from work have very little spare time. If you just sit in front of the television all day you can get old rapidly.

131) Childbirth is a serious business but it is not a disease.

132) Voters are not really interested in political issues except those that effect them directly.

133) Talk to animals much of the time so they know where you are and that you are unthreatening.

134) Never stand behind a coughing cow.

135) Horses can bite as well as kick.

136) Animal matters generate powerful emotions.

137) More people have been proved wrong by saying something is not possible than have said things can be done.

138) Golf and marriage can be difficult subjects to master but the easiest to get advice about.

139) Getting married without any experience is like entering a Grand Prix without a driving licence.

140) Weddings are easy but marriages can be difficult.

141) A great insult to an Englishman is to say that he has no sense of humour.

142) It always seems to come as a surprise to the English that it gets cold in the winter.

143) There is a widely held myth that the sun shines in England continuously from the middle of July to the first two weeks of August. It seldom does.

144) For many snow should only fall on Christmas Day when it is wonderful. Any other time it is quite dreadful for the English.

145) There is more to Switzerland than yodelling and cuckoo clocks, they are not burdened with the EU.

146) Although we in the UK would prefer everyone to drive on the left side of the road, it is as well to conform when the local tradition is to do so on the right.

147) Wine is only fermented grape juice; some is very good grape juice though.

148) It is almost considered to be a mortal sin to be very successful in Great Britain.

149) In the USA the sin is to be unsuccessful.

150) It is hard to understand why some equate sex with being dirty. It is really quite pleasant, sometimes very pleasant indeed.

151) Veterinarians are not failed medical doctors.

152) There is a tide in the affairs of men which taken at the flood, you stand a good chance of getting drowned.

153) The middle of the road position is the one where you are most likely to get run over.

154) When one door closes they can all close.

155) If it isn't one thing it soon is.

156) One way of doing something about being hooked is to cut the line but you can leave the hook in for ever.

157) Try to leave the place better for you having been there.

158) Dogs and other companion animals are better than many people. They are more reliable and they are usually pleased to see you no matter what you have been up to or how much you have drunk at the pub.

159) Sunshine is as dangerous as it is beneficial.

160) Just having all the gear does not make you good at sport.

161) Not paying people on time puts the price of everything up.

162) Call it shoplifting, fiddling, fare dodging, helping yourself to the firms pencils, stationery or whatever without permission (they can afford it), it is still stealing.

163) If you have a white car or a black one, if you wear a dark suit or a grey one that 'doesn't show the dirt', it is still the same dirt, it is still the same dandruff.

164) Silk neckties have a strong attraction for stray food, especially when they are new.

165)   Similarly, the powerful force which drives a gobbet of yoghurt over your best clothes when you open the pot should be harnessed for the good of man.

166)   Coarse jokes can be funny but being filthy is not amusing in itself.

167)   Life does not always have to be fair.

168)   Get on one committee you can get on them all.

169)   The United Kingdom sits in the Atlantic North of all of the USA except Alaska, yet the British resent the fact that it gets cold and wet sometimes.

170)   Money buys many things but contentment is not one of them.

171)   It is better to be nouveau riche than nouveau poor.

172)   If you lose your temper it is likely that you have lost the argument.

173)   Wherever you go in the world and try to take a photograph of your friends in front of the Taj Mahal, Big Ben or the like someone stands in front of you.

174)   Don't drink the tap water and keep out of the sea if you don't want to be ill on holiday abroad.

175)   French cooking can be over-rated but they make very good coffee, bread, cakes and wine. You could live on that I suppose.

176)   The Americans say that the English drink so much tea because of their coffee. In the USA it is the other way round.

177)   Many seaside venues can be awful in the winter, some are like that all the year.

178)   One day it will all go right; one day.

179)   Be careful asking how anyone is. They may start to tell you.

180)   Conscience is often an expression of the fear of being found out.

181)   If you can't grow weeds you can't grow anything.

182) Never be photographed with a drink in your hand. People may get the wrong idea when they see it in the papers on Monday. Worse, they may get the right idea.

183) Common things are common. So look for the simple explanation first.

184) The behaviour of extreme right wing people is often difficult to distinguish from that of extreme left wingers.

185) Local newspapers seem to have a department for changing things to make sure there is something wrong.

186) Write down the location of your vehicle when you leave it in an airport car park. You may think that you will remember but after a few heady days in Tenerife, it can all be blank.

187) You can never find your car if you look in the wrong car park.

188) People who bring pleasure to others don't always get much themselves, especially some famous comedians.

189) Either you both have the dish with garlic or neither has it.

190) If you don't want a dessert don't even look at the sweet trolley.

191) A good test of a work of art is how upset you would be if it went up in smoke. A pile of house bricks, an unmade bed, three tons of rice, a couple of flickering lights are nothing. A Rembrandt or Renoir are irreplaceable.

192) Under no circumstances must you damage any work of art whatever you may think of it.

193) Always set the timer on your video recorder a minute or two either side of the scheduled programme. It is maddening when it cuts out just before the denoument.

194) If you have trouble getting your computer to work get a seven year old to do it for you.

195) It always seems to be people with white cars who park them at right angles to the road so they look like police cars.

196) You don't travel any faster driving only inches from my cars rear bumper.

197) Take the lift (elevator) up and the stairs down.

198) Agendas often seem to self destruct.

199) Diligent canvassing before a meeting can be more effective than a passionate appeal during the proceedings when you are voting on a tricky issue.

200) Everyone with any sense knows that astrology is nonsense. Nevertheless the greatest brains around know their star sign. Many will read their horoscope every day. Maybe there is something in it after all.

201) Cats are the ideal companion animals for modern life. They are idle much of the time, can use the cat flap, they wash themselves, bury their droppings and they don't bark.

202) Anyone can work hard but it is usually the gifted who come up with useful ideas consistently.

203) It is ridiculous as well as inhumane to ship live food animals thousands of miles just to kill them.

204) Describing someone as 'blunt', 'speaks his mind', 'plain speaking', 'forthright' or worst of all 'Does not suffer fools gladly' are all synonyms for 'rude'. Give me someone who does suffer the odd fool any day.

205) Never push anyone into the water.

206) A critique or review of a book, play or film is only an opinion.

207) Weather forecasts are just that. They are forecasts not a factual account of what will happen.

208) Lock your car every time you leave it, even if you are just going in to pay for the petrol (gas).

209) Leave manual vehicles in gear and always leave the handbrake on when stationary.

210) 'Top Secret', 'Private' or 'Confidential' on a document makes it look much more interesting.

211) 'Saying 'Now don't tell anyone this but . . . 'is a sure way of getting it broadcast.

212) House numbers are much easier to find than those with just names.

213) If you were a burglar and came across two houses which looked alike except that one had an alarm system installed and the other did not, which one would you break in?

214) Try calling your house 'Rottweilers' if you don't want unwelcome visitors. An alternative would be to simply stack cans of Pedigree Chum in the window.

215) Newspapers, mail and other items stuck in your letter box advertise you are not at home and will encourage burglars to invite themselves in.

216) Don't buy anything from the door.

217) No-one ever died from copy deadlines, but they can make you very uncomfortable.

218) Surgeons do not always make good carvers of meat.

219) If you pack your umbrella and raincoat it will not rain. Well it will improve your chances.

220) Never pack your lecture slides in the hold luggage on aircraft.

221) Never tell anyone how much money you make unless you have to.

222) Buy books you like as presents for friends well in advance, then you can read them first. Be generous giving but don't let anyone take things from you.

223) If you seek only perfection you will be continuously disappointed. Go for excellence.

224) You only get one chance at a first impression.

225) You can't start with your second operation.

226) When a friend says that their daughter wants to be a veterinarian give them three main points of advice. Get the highest scores you can in the school exams; find out what veterinarians do, not just the local practice but every other department of the profession, go out and get your wellies dirty.

227) Never buy sick looking plants or plants where any look seriously ill.

228) Buy plants with plenty of buds rather than those with lots of blooms.

229) Zebra crossings mean little outside the United Kingdom.

230) Never take risks on the road when there are motor cycles around. They can accelerate at an alarming rate.

231) One of lifes mysteries is why some women get paid good money just for walking up and down a platform in a sulk, wearing a silly frock.

232) You only have one life, as far as we know, so make the most of it.

233) You can't choose your luck.

234) If you and good luck don't meet up very often, make the most of it when they do.

235) Say your name when you are introduced to someone, that will help them remember it.

236) Seeing your name in print is a great boost to the ego, particularly on the shelves of a major bookshop.

237) Tell someone 'That's a good idea' when it is.

238) Stay off alcohol in aircraft, except champagne which is medicinal.

239) Resist getting a personalised car number plate. You don't want the police to remember you do you?

240) The car in front never wants to go as fast as you do. The car behind always wants to push past.

241) There is only one medicine, human medicine is but a part of it.

242) The most effective way of giving up smoking is to boast that you have done so. When offered a cigarette, you say 'No thanks **I** gave it up'.

243) When the Scots stop fighting the English they start fighting each other.

244) Delay listening to the news summary first thing in the morning. It is really only a list of all the bad things that have happened around the world. Play some cheery music instead.

245) Don't make enemies they never do you any good.

246) Politeness is not weakness.

247) Always try politeness first. If that doesn't work review the situation.

248) Drinking alcohol at home alone can be a risky business. It can be pretty hazardous in company but more fun.

249) However big America is the rest of the world is bigger.

250) Learn to work the system before you try to change it.

251) Don't make changes just for the sake of change. Strengthen the good things and improve the less good ones.

252) Many meetings do little more than generate pieces of paper and use up time.

253) Try to hold back at a meeting to assess the company you are in. Then make your point tell.

254) It is usually best not to say anything until you have something to say.

255) You can't edit out the bad bits of your life story. The best thing to do is learn from them and laugh at them if you can.

256) A good story bears repeating, but don't overdo it. Not many people will say they don't want to listen to a Beethoven Symphony or a Mozart opera 'because they've heard it'.

257) Few men have any defence against women in tears.

258) In Ireland it is said that people have two clocks to see if the other one is right.

259) You never see joggers looking happy.

260) The really good guys make it look easy when it isn't, be it football or surgery.

261) Do not persecute moles (*Talpa spp).* Let moley build his District, Circle, Northern and Jubilee underground lines. The more you bully them the more they will modify your garden lawn.

262) Other peoples' gardens always look better from a distance.

263) If you take your address book with you on holiday keep a copy at home. It will be less of a disaster if it goes missing.

264) It is easier to run other peoples' lives than to get a grip on your own.

265) Use your thumb and your second and third fingers when opening tight jars and bottles.

266) Get a cat to mark you with the glands on the side of its face. It will be your friend when it can smell its own secretions. Never push the whiskers forwards.

267) It is a sign of maturity to begin to read the professional journals such as *The Veterinary Record* from the front. The jobs vacant are at the back.

268) If you suffer from insomnia try to remember the very first episode in your life you can put a date to. Then recall the next incident and so on. You will be asleep before your first day at school.

269) If you have a problem blushing when embarrassed, think of the ghastly pictures of concentration camps in wartime or anything else which is gruesome.

270) Playing football in the cricket season could be the explanation for bad weather conditions.

271) The American national sports are similar to netball and rounders, whereas we have cricket.

272) The other difference is that we play with a hard ball. When it comes at you at around 90 miles an hour it can be quite threatening.

273) Your age is not that important, it's how old you are that matters most.

274) I know people half my age who are older than me (no names).

275) When we were students a colleague at College was asked what a cathartic was. He said it is something that makes you cathart.

276) Have the house keys in your hand as you go outside, otherwise sooner or later you will lock yourself out.

277) As you get older you will remember the strict (but not brutal) teachers at school with affection rather than those who were lax.

278) Whatever life hands you, don't take it personally.

279) The height of egotism is to write your own collection of sayings.

280) Most of us males never really grow up.